CELEBRATING FAIZ

جشنِ فیض

CELEBRATING FAIZ

Editor in Chief

D P Tripathi

Chairman

Vichar Nyas Foundation
New Delhi

Vij Books India Pvt Ltd
New Delhi (India)

Published by
Vij Books India Pvt Ltd
(Publishers, Distributors & Importers)
2/19, Ansari Road, Darya Ganj
New Delhi - 110002
Phones: 91-11-43596460, 91-11- 47340674
Fax: 91-11-47340674
e-mail : vijbooks@rediffmail.com
web: www.vijbooks.com

ISBN: 978-93-81411-08-7

Cover designed by and © **Dr. Zoya Zaidi**

CONTENTS

Photographs

INTRODUCTION

Faiz Ahmed Faiz was a poet of romance and revolution. He lived and died writing odes to romance and arousing passion against oppression. He raised his voice and spoke up for the voiceless suffering people and composed some of the finest love poems that adorn Urdu literary tradition. He made adorable his 'Rival in love', his competitor and foe, and sung an ode to him:

"You bring to mind that sheer beauty ...
That beautiful face and those lips
They have filled my dreams, too
Ah, the magical cast of those dreamful eyes
Only you know why I sacrificed my life."

But he ends the *nazm,* embittered and anguished:

"When dignity of labour is sold for naught
When highways thrive with blood of poor
A fire upsurges in my chest
I lose all control over myself."

And then he sings aloud in another nazm:

"We shall witness the day ordained ...
When the crowns will be tossed
When the thrones will be toppled
only Allah will be the reference
Who is absent and present
the spectacle and beholder,
Who is you and I."

Faiz was a lover of life and a fighter for the have-nots and oppressed. And he expressed himself in exquisite Urdu mounted over magical rhythm that touched and overwhelmed every one.

I vividly remember how fondly and with what admiration people surrounded and spoke to him: it was Sheela Sandhu's house in Delhi and the year was 1978 while I was still a student in Jawaharlal Nehru University (JNU). I had read and loved him but had not seen him before.

When I saw him, the words of Mulk Raj Anand about Faiz came rushing to my mind: "Shy, even faced, ... his big eyes seemed to take things to brood upon. He said little." He was completely lost in the atmosphere and seemed eager to listen to every one. When someone pointed out to him that I was a student leader and that I was imprisoned during Emergency for quite some time he looked at me with a deep smile and a conversation ensued. He took an instant liking to me and started calling me *Barkhurdar* (Young Man). It was like a dream coming true for me. Today it is amusing to remember how in the very first meeting we discussed not only Lorca, Nazim Hikmat but also Kalidas, Bhavabhuti and Tulsidas. Faiz had a deep and abiding interest not only in the contemporary world literature but also in ancient literature. When it was time to depart he asked me to come next morning and accompany him to places he was supposed to visit.

The next two days that I spent with him are beyond description. We talked about literature, politics, philosophy, love, passion, folk songs, helplessness, misery ... everything that concerns human life. He specially wanted to know how my life was during imprisonment. I brought to his notice a couplet of mine that I had written in jail:

"Khabar hai ki koi khabar hee nahin hai
Hai dar itna zyada ki dar hee nahi hai"
(The news is that there is no news /
there is so much fear that there is no fear).

He laughed and said, *"Bahut khub, Barkhurdar! Aur likho, likha karo"* (Well done, young man! Write regularly).

Faiz had wanted to keep his visit to Delhi a low-key affair and had mostly abstained from media and public functions, but when I requested him to come to JNU he readily agreed. Kedar Nath Singh has described the event beautifully in his article on Faiz which is being carried in this special issue:

> What I saw that day was totally unprecedented - it was like a minor movement in which almost the entire Delhi was participating. Such

> was the multitude that the last and the tallest person who stood far behind at the end of the crowd was none other than Maqbool Fida Hussain ... It was pure charm of Faiz that had drawn such a huge crowd.

My association with Faiz could only develop further after these few meetings and I met him many times, but the most memorable are the days that he spent with us in Allahabad in 1981. The occasion was his 70th birth day celebration in India. Inder Kumar Gujral was the chairman of the reception committee. All of us participated in the great event. It is unforgettable that outside Delhi, Allahabad was the only city to which he gave two-and-half days at my request. Although distinguished Hindi writer Ravindra Kalia has immortalized that visit, (parts of which have been excerpted in a piece by Ravindra Kalia in this volume) in his book 'Ghalib Chhuti Sharab', I, too, am tempted to share some special memories with Faiz Sahab during his Allahabad sojourn.

After acceding to my request, Faiz Sahab told me: I am going to Allahabad and the foremost desire that I have in me is to meet Firaq Sahab. When I told him that I had already organized that meeting and that it was his first programme in Allahabad, he was extremely pleased. I told him that Firaq Sahab would also be attending his function in the evening. The function was spectacular beyond imagination. The date was 25 April 1981. "The entire city seemed to have turned out towards the university. When Faiz appeared on the stage, the entire campus resounded with the sound of ceaseless clapping... it seemed as if a long lost friend had come back after ages, from across the seven seas."[1] I remember how Faiz Sahab laughed whole-heartedly when Firaq Sahab recited his now famous couplet:

Aane wali naslen tum par rashq karegi hamasron!
Jab unko yah dhyan aayega tumne Firaq ko dekha hai
(The coming generations will envy you
When it will occur to them that you have seen Firaq.)

In two-and-half days Faiz Sahab attended fourteen functions. It was in one of these functions at Hindustani Academy in Allahabad that Shubha Mudgal, who was then Shubha Gupta, a shy young girl, was asked to sing in a high profile function in the presence of Faiz, Mahadevi Verma, Firaq

---

[1] 'When Faiz came to Allahabad' by Ravindra Kalia, pp.198.

and other distinguished writers.

I conducted most of the functions organized during his visit to Allahabad and had the fortune of being his host for a good three hours that he spent at my residence. I had just started teaching in the university and there was hardly anything in my modest flat except two chairs, an ordinary cot and books spread all over. Faiz Sahab looked around and sat on the cot most comfortably. I had, before my eyes a legend sitting like an ordinary human being, without any airs of a celebrity, that he certainly was, he seemed intent on learning as much about folk songs and music that I could tell him. After a while, he lay down but kept the conversation going and keenly followed whatever I had to offer. I remember how he sat up at once, when I explained the meaning of a Sanskrit shloka in context of beauty:

"Kshaney Kshaney Yannavatamupaiti
Tadev rupam ramniyatah"

(One that acquires newness at every moment is beauty).

He remained silent with eyes closed as if soaking in the meaning of 'beauty'. Then I cited how Tulsidas describes Sita's beauty when Lord Rama sees her for the first time in a garden:

"Sundarta kah sundar karaee
chhavi grih deep sikha jimi baraee"

(She makes beauty more beautiful
like a flame aflutter in a house of pictures).

He was overwhelmed. He held my hands and said, "*Barkhurdar, maza aa gaya*" (Young man, you truly entertained me).

There is another great incident that Faiz Sahab precipitated in the last moments of his visit which is hilarious rather than poetic. I had booked his return journey from a mid-night train to Delhi. When I was about to take him to the railway station he told me something which was totally unexpected: *"Barkhurdar, train ko late kara do, hamein Sadiqa Sharan*[2] *se zaroor milna hai* (Young man, you make arrangements to delay the train, I have to meet Sadika Sharan in any case)." Now, this was a bolt from the

[2]. Sadiqa Sharan, wife of eminent lawyer, Shekhar Sharan, and mother of my friend Amar Sharan, now an honourable judge in Allahabad High Court.

blue that left me completely clueless. But saying 'no' to Faiz Sahab was out of question. We rushed to the railway station to plead with the station master. He flatly refused saying 'this is impossible'. We entreated with him endlessly but he remained adamant. Then we gave him the ultimatum that we would all throw ourselves on the track if he did not delay the train. He sensed our desperation and relented. The train was delayed by a good 90-minutes to honour the poet's desire. When he boarded the train, I called up Inder Kumar Gujral in Delhi. He was in deep sleep and it took him a while to understand the cause for Faiz's late arrival.

I remember my mind getting crowded with his *ghazals* and nazms and with the memories of the time spent with the genius as I came out of the railway station. Every human being is unique but there are some who are more unique than others, it is people such as these, who shape history, even as it shapes them. Faiz Ahmed Faiz was perhaps among this category of great men whose life and works are the inspiring script of the struggle, for a better future for all, commitment to principals of equity and justice and above all, overwhelming love for humanity.

Faiz lives through his poetry as one of the most beautiful poets of 'beauty'.

(D. P. Tripathi)

Faiz Ahmed 'Faiz', Mahadevi Verma & Raghupati Sahay 'Firaq'
25 April, 1981, Senate House Lawns, Allahabad University

Faiz Ahmed Faiz

Long Live Gandhiji*

The British tradition of announcing the death of a king is "The king is dead, long live the king!"Nearly 25 years ago, Mahatma Gandhi writing a moving editorial on the late CR Das in his exquisite English captioned it as "Deshbandhu is dead, long live Deshbandhu!" If we have chosen such a title for our humble tribute to Gandhiji, it is because we are convinced, more than ever before, that very few indeed have lived in this degenerate century, who could lay greater claim to immortality than this true servant of humanity and champion of the downtrodden. An agonizing 48 hours (sic) at the time of writing this article, have passed since Mahatma Gandhi left this mortal coil. The first impact of the shock is slowly spending itself out, and through the murky mist of mourning and grief, a faint light of optimistic expectation that Gandhiji has not died in vain, is glowing. Maybe it is premature to draw such a conclusion now in terms of net result, but judging by the fact that the tragedy has profoundly stirred the world's conscience, we may be forgiven, if we lay store by the innate goodness of the man. At least we can say, at the top of our voices, to suspicious friends in India that the passing away of Gandhiji is as grievous a blow to Pakistan as it is to India. We have observed distressed looks, seen moistened eyes and heard faltering voices in this vast sprawling city of Lahore, to a degree only to be seen to be believed. We have also seen spontaneous manifestations of grief on the part of our fellow citizens in the shape of observance of a holiday and *hartal*. Let our friends in India take note and we declare it with all the emphasis at our command, that we in Pakistan are human

---

* Faiz wrote this editorial for *The Pakistan Times* dated 02 February, 1948, a day after Gandhiji's assassination.

enough to respond to any gesture of goodwill, any token of friendliness and, last but not the least, any call for cooperation from the other side of the border. Earlier we have indulged in a bit of optimism and that too for a very good reason. In India, sedulous and we believe sincere, heart searching has been going on ever since the tragedy took place. The Government of India too seems to have at long last realised that they are sitting on top of a volcano. And above all, a small incident in Bombay in which a Hindu mob broke open the office of the Anti-Pakistan Front on Saturday and reduced its furnishings to smithereens is, we believe, the realisation though tragically belated, of the fact that Muslims are, after all, not the sinners, not to say the enemies of India. A large section of Hindus have discovered where their enemies reside and what political labels they flaunt. Not long ago, at Lucknow, India's Deputy Prime Minister, Sardar Patel, while hauling nationalist Muslims, who had assembled there a few days earlier, over the coals, sang a paean of praise for RSS and the Hindu Mahasabha - the organisation which, alas, produced that worst criminal in history, Nathuram Vinayak Godse. Sardar Patel pandered to their jingoistic vanity by asking the Congress to flirt with them. Paradoxical though it may seem, his chief, Pandit Nehru, while at Amritsar, two days prior to the tragedy, picked the RSS and Sabha bubbles in no uncertain manner by describing their politics as doing the greatest harm to the country. Again, just one day after the pledge given by representatives of different political organisations to Gandhiji, for the promotion of communal amity, which led him to break his fast, the well-known Hindu Mahasabha leaders Mr. Deshpande and Prof. Ramsingh, had the temerity to say that Muslims must be driven out of India. If the Government of India would have tried to take some of the conceit and "fire" out of these rabidly communal and militant leaders, maybe Gandhiji would have lived to be 125. Instead of planting bombs and other weapons in innocent Muslims' houses in Delhi and other parts of India, had Mr. Patel's intelligence department taken good care to protect the precious life of Mahatmaji, this vast subcontinent, as indeed the world, would not have been smitten "by this calamity". It was far from us to recount these pre-tragedy happenings but we feel constrained to do so for the weighty reason that the destiny of fifty million Muslims is involved in India. We demand that the powers that be in India, must treat them fairly and squarely. We would be less than human if we were to make even the least attempt to exploit Gandhiji's death in furtherance of our co religionists' interests in India. But we are gratefully conscious of the fact that nothing would give greater pleasure to the soul of the illustrious dead than dispensation of justice and fair play to Indian Muslims, which he so passionately preached and for which he laid down his life. To these countless Muslims, Mahatmaji would ever remain a symbol of hope and courage. Though he is dead, he will live through ageless life.

Inder Kumar Gujral*

With my teacher Faiz

This memoir is of historic importance since it contains a reliable account of Faiz's life, his creative journey and the various stages of his struggle. Though Gujral was his student during college days, later they became intimate friends. Gujral had very close relations with Faiz at a personal level and he is also deeply attached to his poetry - Editor.

I vividly remember that it was the winter of early December and the year was 1983 when I was invited to attend an international conference in Islamabad. The extreme attraction to visit my old country and meet old pals took me there for three weeks. But the journey did not quench my thirst. I came back more thirsty.

My relation with Lahore is special because I spent a major part of my youth in the lanes and roads of this city-the same old university building, the same college and hostel, the same bungalow of our in-laws where our marriage was solemnized. The memories of that evening flooded my mind when Faiz and Mazhar Ali were among the baaratis. Even Faiz had not forgotten it. As he met my wife he asked 'You have been to our house, haven't you?'

The historic Bredla Hall and Lajpat Rai Bhavan were also there in Lahore. Majaz had once said about them:

> We understood the meaning of suffering and freedom here
>
> It was here that we whipped up our passion
>
> And sang songs of love

---

* Inder Kumar Gujral, one of India's highly respected political leaders and a former Prime Minister of India.

And it was this obsession that caused my meeting with Faiz. As the conference in Islamabad got over, we reached Lahore via Peshawar. We had already spoken to each other over phone. Both Alys and Faiz reached our hotel as soon as they came to know of our arrival. They had invited us for a stay at their house but we could not go there because they were situated on the outskirts of Model Town and we wanted to stay at a place where we could meet as many friends as possible. Also, there was this keen desire to traverse the familiar roads and lanes. Faiz readily understood our compulsions and agreed.

At that time, the Indian cricket team was also there in Lahore. Our high-commissioner Humayun Kabir was hosting a dinner for them. As soon as it became known to him that Alys and Faiz were in our room, he arrived with his contingent. He had not met Faiz before. They got introduced to each-other and all of us went to the party. The party was for teetotalers. Kababs were available but Pakistani prohibition laws were very stringent. Faiz endured soft drinks, like coca-cola, for long.

Since Moscow, I was meeting Faiz after two years. His face was a bit pale and his steps had also slowed down. I asked Alys the reason. She said that doctors had apprehensions about his heart, but now he was sure of himself and that he was chain-smoking as usual. That was not the first time that doctors had advised him restraint. Doctors had admitted him in a hospital once, in Moscow, as well. However, that was good for him because Doctor Z.A. Ahmed, Hajra Begum and P.C. Joshi were also there at that time and they enjoyed each other's company in the hospital. Once he told me on phone, "Brother, when you come, please do not forget about my thirst." I replied, "You are behaving strangely, doctors have strongly advised you not to drink". "Brother, you are great, doctors have forbidden me, but not you." Ironically, when he died, he had given up drinking for almost an year and those who had met him in London, were of the opinion that he looked healthier and better.

Next evening we went to his house for dinner. Alys had invited only her daughters and sons-in-law. Salima and Muniza had earlier come to our house when they were very young. Now they had lovely children. Faiz produced Indian whisky. I was surprised. I asked, "How come? I have heard that law enforcement agency sends officers even inside homes. How have you managed Indian whisky?" "Everything is fine, sir. I am not the one to obey such orders."

There was a joke doing rounds in Karachi at that time that drinking alone is more dangerous because under Zia's regime even the walls had eyes. But it was easier in a bigger parties, provided one had invited some army officers also. That day our conversation veered mostly around political issues - Indo-Pak relations in the changed scenario, how Russia's entry into Afghanistan had impacted different persons in differing ways. The Leftists were not alarmed. Rather, they believed that had Pakistan not been America's puppet, it could have prevented the break up of the socialist regime. There was another dominant school of thought which believed that in the changed scenario, Pakistani Progressive Organisations should work for better relations with India. This was the time when Faiz had just returned form Beirut. The plight of the people there had deeply impacted him. His nazms of those days gave voice to their pain and sufferings. That evening, we listened to his 'lullaby' for the Palestinian children.

We had only recently organised his 70th birth anniversary in Delhi. Faiz's son-in-law Hashmi told us that this had a very deep impact on the people of Pakistan. "People kept talking of democratic and liberal Indian society for months. Many had even made cassettes of that Indian TV programme. But what happened here? Faiz was away. A birth Anniversary Committee was set up. As soon as the news got published, all the members of the committee, along with me, were arrested and we spent the birthday, in the dirty cells of Old Anarkali Police Station."

He went on to say, "there happened an interesting incident in the police station. For reasons unknown, the police had arrested a young Maulvi along with us. He was crying bitterly and was repeating that he was a supporter of General Sahib and that he was mistakenly caught. Someone among us said that all of us were supporters of Zia Sahib and that yesterday night some army officers ousted Zia Sahib. That's why his supporters are getting caught." The constable standing outside, was listening. He rushed to tell the inspector. The inspector soon rang somebody. When he was scolded, he came to us and said, "your joke almost destroyed my career. Thankfully the officer was obliging." That was our last meeting. The next day we returned to Delhi. A year before I had written to him to participate in the Ambala mushayra but he suffered a heart attack. Mazhar sent the news of his illness and he also sent the *nazm* which he had written in Mev Hospital. As usual it contained pathos and resolution:

It seems I have hit a dead end, there is nothing for me now
Neither the moon, nor the sun, neither darkness, nor light ...

Faiz's poetry contains depths of agony as well as courage and resolution which always inspires us towards hope. Years of imprisonment and the fear that he will be hanged, could not discourage him, rather they adorned his poetry:

Pearl, crystal, goblet
Once broken is broken
Tears cannot mend it,
It's lost if broken.
You gather the shards
Save them for naught
There is no Messiah of Crystals,
What good is your hope?

However, the beauty of his poetry lies in the fact that behind this sadness and disappointment, there is a story of immense struggle which he expresses in his own inimitable, exquisite language. His romanticism and revolution radicalised the whole of our generation. Now the memory of all that seems so very old. The Second World War was going on. It was difficult to guess whether Hitler would win or lose. Those were the last years of my student life. But the political turmoil took precedence over our studies. I was with the left-politics and so we were imprisoned. People like us had political dreams, which went beyond mere independence. Therefore, our discourse often centered around contemporary social-literary issues and revolution. The Progressive Writers' Movement was also emerging in those days. Among the new writers, the unique writing style of Faiz was being talked about the most.

All of a sudden we came to know that Faiz was moving from Amritsar and coming to Lahore, to our own college, as lecturer of English literature. We were surprised because ours was not only a government college but our principal also was an Englishman. But he (Principal) was an open minded person, he sympathized with the freedom movement and therefore, perhaps, he had no qualms regarding the selection of Faiz. I had an indirect introduction to him to some extent but soon our relations transcended the limits of teacher-pupil relation and the foundation of a long lasting friendship was laid down.

Youthful days have many attractions and fantasies and for us, revolution signified many things. It included patriotism and the will to change the social system. Therefore Faiz's poetry was representative of our emotional debates and used to touch us deeply. There was not a single colleague or friend who did not remember 'Naksh-e-Fariyadi' or who did not talk of *Mujhse pehli si muhabbat mere mehboob na maang.*

The greatest attraction of Faiz was his simple language. Codwell's 'Studies in Dying Culture' was published during those days. I can still recall the foreword in which he has said that poetry is romance also because it is linked to language and society, inseparably. Faiz has reproduced the same in his own style. John Freeman's autobiography 'New Testament' was also being debated during those days and it had caused disturbing ripples among left wing supporters. Freeman used to be a communist, but he gave up communism. Since he was also a poet, people had differing opinions about him. One incident of his life has been beautifully described. During his university days, he met a beautiful girl, who asked him what he would do after college. He said 'Poetry and Revolution'. Though the girl liked the idea very much, she thought it prudent to marry another happy youth. Faiz too had embraced 'Poetry and revolution', but he had better fortune. It really seemed strange when we got the news that he was marrying an English woman, without going to England. But Faiz had his speciality even in that. Alys had come to Amritsar to meet her sister Mrs. Tasir and there she met Faiz. Their like mindedness drew them close to each other and made their love everlasting. By the time Faiz came to Lahore, Tasir Sahab had moved to Srinagar as principal, so that the marriage took place there and the 'Niqah' was read by the late Sheikh Abdullah. Sheikh Sahab often dwelt on that later on. All the big leaders of Kashmir National Front came to attend the marriage ceremony. Faiz's friendship with Sadiq Sahab and Bakshi Gulam Muhammad started at that time only. God had showered many blessings on Faiz. But a wife like Alys is truly rare. The way she has sailed through difficult times is a testimony of her commendable courage.

When the Axis power led by Hitler seemed to be gaining upper hand in the war, leftists and some thinker friends started feeling that defeating Nazi barbarism was the foremost objective and in the eventuality of Hitler's victory, the progressive and revolutionary forces would disintegrate. This motivation took sentimental people like Faiz and Mazhar Ali to the army and Faiz came to Delhi, having resigned from the college. I had moved to Karachi after completing my studies. I came to Delhi for a short while. New Delhi used to be very different during those days. Nights used to be blacked out. And it was a forest area across the India Gate. Faiz's house was in Lodhi Estate. I had accepted his invitation for dinner but reaching there on tonga, turned out to be a major difficulty. Now Faiz Sahib had only two options - either he could drop me in his old Austin car or make some arrangements for my stay.

Partition altered everything. Having been exiled, we came to Delhi. Faiz went back to Lahore. For some years, we lost touch with each other. Now, there was a new phase in Faiz's life. Miyan Iftkharuddin had launched 'Pakistan Times' and 'Imroj'. Faiz and Mazhar Ali were appointed Editor and Joint Editor respectively. When we heard this news, we felt proud to be his friends. Here in India our days and nights were being spent in the pursuit of ration cards and allotment of houses. When Ayub Khan assumed power, the government of Pakistan confiscated 'Pakistan Times' and 'Imroj'. They are still government trust properties. Soon Rawalpindi Conspiracy case was fabricated. Faiz and Sajjad Zaheer were arrested and imprisoned. After some time Miyan Iftkharuddin died. He was a very rich man during his time. He became a revolutionary while studying in Oxford. When he returned he established close relations with Jawaharlal Nehru who was the then Punjab Congress president. He had very intimate relations with Faiz, Mahmood Ali, Mazhar Ali and some other leftist people like us. Faiz was deeply aggrieved at his demise. After coming out from the jail he expressed his pain through a beautiful elegy.

The politics in India was taking a new turn at that time. Congress was getting divided. The day Indira Gandhi was expelled from the party, I sent her a couplet of Faiz. She liked it very much. Though she was never a master in remembering Urdu couplets, she would often ask me 'What was that couplet of Faiz ?'

Faiz had close relations with both Panditji and Indiraji. In 1955, when Faiz came to Delhi, Panditji spent an entire evening with him. After 1971, the situation in Pakistan changed drastically. During Bhutto's regime, Faiz was appointed the Director of National Arts Council and he visited Delhi in that connection. I was Information and Broadcasting Minister then. He asked me to do two things - first, send Shila Bhatia's famous Opera 'Heer Ranjha' to Pakistan, and second, organise an exhibition of the photographs taken by my brother Satish Gujral. I said that, as a principle, there could be no objection. But we put a condition that he would have to present a programme on Delhi TV. Faiz Sahib delivered his promise, but neither Shila Bhatia's Opera nor Satish Gujral could go to Pakistan. Such were the relations between the two countries those days. Bhutto also had begun to change colours. Faiz was getting despondent because of that. He was among those who felt that Bhutto's mistakes were paving ways for army rule. But this was destined. In India also, history turned itself and Emergency was imposed. Initially he thought that the Emergency was imposed only to break leftism but soon he realized the design and intentions behind the imposition. When we met, Faiz spoke sarcastically. He lamented that instead of bringing Pakistan on the democratic path, India herself had slipped back.

With the advent of General Zia's regime, the same old days of suffocation and harassment of intellectuals, returned to haunt. Faiz somehow escaped to Moscow but Alys and the children had to face hardships for very long. By then Emergency had pushed me, too, to Moscow. When we met, our friendship, and his *nazm* 'Mere Dil Mere Musafir' went straight into my heart. I benefited a lot from his company in Moscow. Every evening he would find time to be with us. We often organised poetic gatherings to which High Commissioners of Pakistan and Bangladesh would also come. Faiz had many admirers in Russia, who had seen another aspect of life through his poetry. Urdu language is indeed indebted to Faiz for making it an international language.

There is another story. Our famous Hindi Poet, Harivansh Rai Bachchan had come to Moscow. A *Mushayra* took place in the evening. Faiz also played his role beautifully. I still remember the beautiful couplet that he recited that day:

I made my life simple / I only loved

During his stay in Moscow, he was appointed Editor of Alamgir Magazine Lotus. He went to Beirut and stayed there for long. Alys also arrived after some time. The destruction of Beirut left a deep impression on his poetry:

Today also the moon did not come
how much had I wanted it to come

It is difficult to believe that Faiz would have passed away silently. He must have asked the Death God:

Could you show me my death warrant
I wanted to see whose seal it bears

I would like to narrate an incident before concluding. Mahmood Zafar and Rasheed Jahan played pivotal roles, in shaping Faiz's poetry. The second phase of his poetry took him from the 'lanes of the beloved' to the 'guillotine.' I remember receiving his message when later I went to Moscow - 'Pay homage on the grave of Rasheed Jahan on my behalf also.' In the freezing cold of December, my wife and I, found out the grave of Rasheed Jahan and paid floral tributes on his behalf.

Faiz was primarily a poet, but he was also a loving friend and a beautiful human being. The vacuum that he has left, will never be filled.

Kuldip Nayar*

Faiz remains a beacon of light ...

We, half a dozen Indian journalists, were having lunch in a hotel in Moscow when Faiz Ahmed Faiz, in a suit and necktie, entered the dinning hall. The entrance was at the farthest end of our table. I got up from my chair and asked my colleagues to do the same. "Here comes the greatest Urdu poet of the Indian sub-continent", I said, when he was approaching us, seeing a clutch of young men standing.

I had never met Faiz before, not even at Sialkot, home town for both of us. Probably the best of the Sialkotees flourished outside Sialkot. Faiz spoke Punjabi with the Sialkotee accent. He was touchy about his Urdu pronunciation, which was made fun of, in Urdu circles, and he told me that he gave up Urdu poetry for some time to switch over to Punjabi. He once made a much-talked about trip to Lucknow, to meet the poet, Majaz Lakhnawi, who would say 'Ji han' (Yes please), while Faiz replied 'Han ji, Han ji', in the typical way Punjabis say 'yes'.

I had seen photos of Faiz and that was how I recognized him. Although I had read his poetry, being an Urdu and Persian graduate myself, I appreciated it better after meeting him. He shook hands with each of us and said smilingly: Moscow is a beautiful city. See every part of it before you return to India. He did not stay long but struck up an acquaintance, which helped me come near him in the following years.

He would visit Delhi almost every six months. Referring to our meeting at Moscow, I was able to meet him at Delhi. All the days when he was in the city, he spent the evenings with one friend or the other. They too, awaited his return anxiously. It was the pick of the society before which he would recite his poetry long after mid-night. Sheela and Hali Vats, my friends, were his permanent hosts. They would invite to their modest house

---

* Kuldip Nayar is a distinguished journalist, former Indian High Commissioner to United Kingdom and former Member of Parliament (Rajya Sabha).

the leading artists, academicians, and poets, but correctly avoided politicians. What came to be known as "Sham-e-Faiz" was not confined to the invites. He was like a flower which attracted bees from all over. Many would gatecrash the place and stand in some corner, because the floor would be filled with the admirers, squatting before him.

Faiz and I became friends but avoided any discussion on politics. Once when I went to Pakistan, to interview the then Prime Minister Zulfikar Ali Bhutto, I exchanged views on the happenings in Pakistan. This was after the liberation of Bangladesh. He blamed nobody but regretted that one portion of Pakistan was no more its part. He was then a member of Bhutto's delegation. He was hurt by the stories of atrocities that he had heard from Dhaka. He recited to me the first couplet of the poem that he wrote after his visit to Bangladesh:

And will there be a spring when the green is all unblighted

And how many rains must fall before the spots are washed clean

Once he talked at Lahore about radical Islam. Since he was a Leftist but not an atheist, he argued how Islam and the ideology of the Left, were on the same page. 'Lal Islam' is the phrase he used. I was amazed at his observation but then he spoke with such passion and conviction that I kept quiet. His desire to have an egalitarian society was known through his poetry but his coinage of 'Lal Islam', was not.

Many years after his death, one of his poems became the freedom cry of the suppressed Pakistanis against the regime of general Zia-ul-Haq. I was present at the Shimla Pahari at Lahore, when thousands of men and women, particularly the youth, joined Iqbal Bano singing the famous poem by Faiz. Words fail me to describe the frenzy and the defiance which the words evoked.

We shall witness

It is certain that we too, shall witness

the day that has been promised

of which has been written on the slate of eternity

When the enormous mountains of tyranny

Will blow away like cotton
When under our feet- the feet of the oppressed-
the earth will pulsate deafeningly
and lightning will crackle strike down
above the heads of the rulers

From the abode of God
When icons of falsehood will be taken out,
When we- the faithful- who have been banished from sacred places
will be enthroned
When the crowns snatched,
And thrones will be toppled

Only The name of God will survive
The God who is unseen but also present
Who is the spectacle and the beholder, both
I am the Truth- the cry will rise,
Which is I, as well as you
And then God's creation will rule
Which is I, as well as you

Iqbal Bano, who rendered the poem, was arrested for violating a British law (of 1888) under which the poetry of Faiz, in Pakistan, had been banned. Still Zia could not keep out the song from the psyche of Pakistan because it was a cry for freedom. For months, everyone hummed it to voice protest.

Today, after 26 years, (the poem was sung in 1985) Zia is remembered as a military dictator, who not only killed hundreds of Pakistanis but also introduced fundamentalism, for which the people in Pakistan are paying a heavy price.

Faiz remains a beacon of light and his poem, 'Hum Dekhenge', shines every dark nook and corner of the world where oppression prevails. Even in India, where democracy is entrenched, the victims of oppression as well as poverty, cry in their own way, in their own language 'hum dekhenge'.

Mulk Raj Anand*

Reminiscences of Faiz Ahmed Faiz

Shy, even-faced young man, with curly hair, his big eyes seemed to take things in, to brood upon. He said little. He moved slowly. But, suddenly, during a meal, or when passing one by from one room to another, he would recite a verse, either of some older poet, or the beginning of a new one of his own. Often we shared Ghalib's tormented utterance in the *mushaira* of Bahadur Shah Zafar:

> Oh innocent heart, what has happened to you?

In fact, this became our greeting to each other for years, whenever we met. And we would smile away the agony.

I first met Faiz in the house of Dr Muhammad Din Taseer, whom I had known in Cambridge and London, in his house, off Lawrence Road, Amritsar, when he was Principal of the Islamic College, in my home-town. Faiz was lecturer in English in the college and stayed with Taseer. Christabel, the English wife of the Principal, was known to me, when she had worked with my Quaker publisher, Sir Stanley Unwin, as also we had been meeting daily in Taseer's digs in Belsize Park, in the loose group we had formed of the Progressive Writers' Association, with Sajjad Zaheer, Dr Ghosh, Iqbal Singh, Taseer, Harkirat Singh, Victor Kiernan and Som Nath Chib. Chris was our hostess and invariably cooked chicken curry, Punjab style, as I had taught her. And she was learning Urdu from her husband so that she might not feel completely out of our confabulations and poetry recitals. Her assiduity helped her when she came to stay in Amritsar and she won many people over, who thought Taseer should not have brought a 'Mem' home. She was very fond of Faiz. We both thought Faiz resembled Rimbaud, the

---

* Late Mulk Raj Anand was a leading figure in the Progressive Writers' Movement and an eminent writer.

French boy-poet, who had become the rage of the twenties, in England, after Edgell Rickward wrote a biography of this wizard of startling, defiant words.

In many ways, this likeness of Faiz to Rimbaud, found by Chris and myself, has proved to be apt. Both were near villagers, from modest families, whose genius was nourished by the revolt against the repression of the instinctive life in the patriarchal set up, over which was the bigger patriarch, the monarch, lorded over by the big-bearded Almighty God sitting in heaven, above the skies. Both began to protest early. And, going against the conventional time spirit, they both faced the human predicament, with awakening words, discarding the conventional ritual-ridden faiths, by thought-breaking images, abandoning the fatalism of the previous bards, and becoming visionaries by default.

The poet is the conveyer of imperceptible stirrings, of liquid aspirations, of feeling towards expression of inner awareness, inspired by the conflict of relative innocence with experience. He notices the decay of previous images through too much use. And he finds the contraries of daily life, through people's acceptance of old bad habits, against his own passion for truth to be reaching out to the inner fire, 'burning and melting ever, like the moth on the flame,' as Jalal-ud-din Rumi said after writing the *mathnavi.*

I felt, during my stays with Taseer and Chris, in close contact with Faiz, every second year, whether in Amritsar, Srinagar or Lahore, that he was unconsciously akin not only to Rimbaud, but to the English imagists, Laura Riding, D.H. Lawrence, Richard Aldington, the French Aragon, Eluard and Tzara and the Latin American Pablo Neruda.

As I recall the atmosphere of that time, I realize that most of the poets of integrity were 'thieves of fire', in Rimbaud's sense of those words. They seemed to hear the sighs which rose from the smouldering ashes of discontent against sufferings imposed by men on other men, the oppression of the old decaying forms. And they uttered the truth about the injustice they saw of the rich towards the poor. In this way, the various expressions of our time, found a universal validity by echoing the passionate yearning for a possible future of hope for man's survival, on some planes of integrity, against the blanket oppression, which was visible in the marching of goose-stepping armies.

In our casual talks at the table, (I remember several of these exchanges in the small dining-room of the house-boat in which we lived one summer with Taseer, by the Bund on the Jhelum river in Srinagar) we often talked of Allama Iqbal, who had shown the way to the recognition of the human situation.

In fact, to transmit to the young children of the house, the message of Iqbal, Faiz wrote out, on a poster, Allama's poem of pity for the orphan of the storm and poor peasants of the Punjab. In one small *mushaira*, on top of the boat, Taseer recited Iqbal's hymn to Lenin. And Faiz matched that utterance with Iqbal's opening up of new worlds, by repeating the first few lines of the poem, in which Allama said:

> Beyond the stars there are other worlds
>
> There are more trials on the path of love to come
>
> You are the falcon, whose work is to fly.
>
> Before you, there are still other skies to soar over ...

I was reading Arnold Toynbee's 'Study of History' at that time, and I read out to the family gathering, this visionary's words: 'For our first million years, we, human race fought lions and tigers to win a future for our ascendents. Thirty thousand years ago, we won an ascendency over all non-human nature, except bacteria. Since then, we have had only two enemies, microbes and men...'

This prompted a reading of some passages from an article by Jawaharlal Nehru on the 'Ultimate purpose of men's life.'

Taseer, Faiz and I, discussed the need for a big get-together of writers as soon as we reached Lahore. We felt that our poets must break away from the sentimental ghazal and make reality our *mehbooba* (beloved). The mechanical manipulation of verse from *Kafia* to *Kafia* was also to go. Our poetry and prose must derive strength from the confrontation of human realities, not only of our freedom struggle, but against the dethronement of humanness by the genocide which the oppressors were boastfully announcing to the world, as their answer to the revolt of the masses against the yoke of Imperialist, Fascist and militarist tough-necks. Only when man may seek to become a whole man through all his concrete experience of suffering, can writing become genuine in content and beautiful in form. So we felt.

In Faiz's poems of that period, the beloved became the symbol of Revolution. The nostalgia for the beloved with her kiss curls, as in the romantic Urdu poetry, and in the paintings of Chugtai, gave place to the beloved as in Mayakovsky's fiery verse. Only, unlike Mayakovsky, Faiz did not write poster verse, but a new kind of melodious *ghazal*, with onomatopoeic words, used as symbols for new beginnings.

There had come to us, an uncanny sense of the doomsday among people in the West, in the late thirties, when I returned to London in 1933. I saw a disillusioned people, who, having suffered under successive conservative governments, from want through mass-unemployment, were being offered jobs in Arms' factories. The upper hierarchies in Britain and France were trying to find ways and means to appease the Fascists to rebuild their navy. They said they were making up for the humiliation of the Germans in the coach, where the Versailles treaty was signed. The future of human beings later became the focus for the eyes, hearts and minds of the creative men and women of the whole world, in what has been called the 'thirties' movement'.

The Progressive Writers of India, inspired by Tagore, Iqbal and Jawaharlal Nehru, became intimately involved in the struggle against violence of the fascists, aping their elder cousins, the Imperialists, and asking for lebensraum.

In the World Writers' Conference in Paris, in early 1936, inaugurated by Maxim Gorky, with Andrè Malraux, Aragon, as the prime movers, the fatalists who believed in 'pure' art without involvement in human, especially political affairs, were won over to declarations against the murderers of hope.

In the anti-fascist writers' campaign in UK, I was put on the platform as representative of India in late 1936. I read out a message from Jawaharlal Nehru, asking for the weak to be defended, the Herrenvolk theory of superior races negated, and the conscience of men and women kindled into awakening, through the words of the poets. The enemies of life took advantage of the cynicism of the owners of world space.

General Franco, with the help of the 'super heroes', Hitler and Mussolini, attacked, with hired Moorish gangs, the popular Government elected in Spain under Cabalero, a working man. The curtain-raiser for the Second World War was enacted.

Most of the forward anti-fascist writers of the West did what writers had seldom done before, unless recruited by their will, they joined the Republican army.

In consultation with my colleagues in the Progressive Writers' Movement, who had met in Lucknow under the chairmanship of Prem Chand, I went to Spain and joined the International brigade with Andrè Malraux, Ralph Fox, John Cornford, Christopher Caudwell, Arturo Baria and others.

Although we had been aware, in the poems of Tagore, Iqbal, Vallathol, Bharati and the younger writers Nirala, Faiz, Bishnu Dey, Jafri and Majaz, of the sense of shock, at the barbarism released by the masters, against the slaves of violence, against the Gandhian non-violence, few of us were actually aware of the organised oppression, through the killing of six million Jews by Hitler in Germany, and we had not grasped the methods of the ruthless, impersonal, centralized, uniformed jackboot armies of oppression, recruited on the parallel of the previous Imperialist armies, by the marauders of democracy. Those, like the Bolsheviks, who realized the subversion of people's rights, reacted, under Stalin, by also attempting an anomic mechanics of revolutionary force, which became a huge violent force to confront violence.

The feeling that I was going against the vow I had taken to be non-violent from Gandhiji, acted in me, strangely enough, as I fainted on seeing a wounded man bleeding in Dr Bethune's surgery in Barcelona during the Spanish war. I asked to be put in the category of journalists, near the trenches, as I felt I could not shoot anyone, even an enemy.

I must confess, I reverted back to the feeling that a writer cannot act out his words. I recalled that, in the primitive societies, the bard was never asked to fight, but invited to sing about the war because he was physically weak, gentle and timid. The creative writer in our age has to suffer from the schizoid sense of alienation from the mass, because, often, he cannot actively participate from his heart in the new global culture of armed struggle, that is war.

Of course, quite a few western writers died fighting in Spain, including our friends, John Cornford, Ralph Fox, Christopher Caudwell and David Guest. Andrè Malraux fought thoughout. And there was hardly any significant poet or novelist of the major modern literatures, from Hemingway to Neruda and Alberti, who were not present at the Anti-Fascist Conference in Madrid, in the spring of 1937.

The protagonists of the culture of war, however, stormed the Republican trenches, with weapons from Nazi Germany and Fascist Italy. The new mechanics of the coming Second World War were tried out in Spain. And Franco won.

I returned to India to end my schizophrenia, of wanting to struggle, but being held back by the Gandhian sentiments I had imbibed, aspiring to non-violence but unable to avoid the temptation of resorting to violence.

I recall that most of us lived in this schizoid sense of unreality. I met my mentor, Jawaharlal Nehru, and my old friends, Sajjad Zaheer, Muhammad Din Taseer, Faiz Ahmed Faiz, Hiren Mukherji and Bishnu Dey. We had all been dumbed by the shock of the defeat in Spain. We were aware that those who had won the empire with machine guns and gunboats, as also those who had perfected, through Krupp and Schneider, new instruments of war, beyond those used in the Imperialist war machines, had unconcealed contempt for Gandhi's non-violent campaigns. Our physical weakness was seen as our moral weakness. We were 'lower breeds beyond the law.'

We organised gatherings all over India to reassert our belief in the culture of humanism.

It was reassuring to find that Faiz's poetry showed no sign of despair, though he seemed to acknowledge defeat. And he inspired the young writers to face themselves. The poem of Majaz, 'Awara', is not so much the confession of a vagabond, but the protest of the disinherited against the patriarchs, who were supporting the suzerainty of the King Emperor from their big houses in Oudh.

In the evenings, spent together in the house of a Brown Baron turned egalitarian, Mian Iftikhar-ud-Din, with *saqi* plying the liquor, there were always recitals of new poems, often by Faiz. But we also talked about the new phenomena of pragmatic atheists like Jinnah, posing as the heroes of Islam - the man had never read the Koran even in English. The Taluqdars of Oudh, knowing that the nationalists of India may divide their vast lands among the poor, had visions of owning thousands of acres of the fertile earth of West Punjab. They exalted the pseudo-heroes of the Muslim League. Under the new suzerainty of the Qaide-Azam, there would be opportunities for 'Junkers' to grow. The Muslim merchants of Bombay and Calcutta would bring the necessary investment for the industries. Faiz understood the unscrupulous egoism of the so-called Muslim leaders, who had never said a prayer, except on Id Day, who were political stooges, often, of the Imperial power, encouraging unfettered hate against the 'Hindu Bania Gandhi' and his followers, invoking the words of Churchill to condemn the 'naked fakir'.

'From the strife of the lower orders, a higher order of the elite could get the fruits of victory,' said Taseer almost in a whisper one evening. And he invoked Iqbal's idea of 'The will might bring enlightenment. Even the Jinnahs might get light'. We felt he had turned away from us.

Slowly, after this kind of talk, Faiz and I were estranged from Taseer. And during the years, the separation became long absences from each other, Faiz had already married Chris's sister, Alys.

With the help of Sajjad Zaheer, Hiren Mukherji and Abdul Aleem, I organised the Progressive Writers Conference in Calcutta in 1938, where Rabindranath Tagore sent a Presidential Address. The old poet talked of the threat to human civilization through the machinations of the Fascists, of the need to modernize consciousness, to become fully aware of the new found ones.

Jawaharlal Nehru sympathised with us. He was aware, like Tolstoy and Gandhi, of the way in which the neo-heroes created artificial feelings in the people, which they do not possess if they are left to themselves, but which seize them, like the cry, 'Religion in danger', a hysteria uttered by the heroes. He said it needed renascent thinking to go beyond the wars of the 'Reformation', to separate religion from politics. He was sympathetic to Julian Huxley's evolutionary humanism. And he asked me to sit down somewhere quietly and write on this theme-how ritual was being passed off as religion, and communal riots being organised to murder, by throwing a cow's head in a temple and a pig's head in a mosque.

I thought I would go to London, pack up my books and return soon to start a culture centre in Lahore.

I had hardly finished a new novel to earn some royalties to pay my fare back, when Hitler attacked Poland. At last the Patriarchs who had appeased Hitler in Munich and Prague and Vienna had to put up a stand. The Soviets, knowing that the West was soft to the fascists, hoping they would turn East certainly, for lebensraum, called it an 'Imperialist war'. In fact, machine was to answer machine. So they bought time with a pseudo-pact with Hitler. All ideologies were broken. All heroes became Madame Tussaud's sensational wax dummies. All the world entered a dark age.

I opted to be a conscientious objector and was condemned to till an acre of land, until Krishna Menon, as Alderman in the Camden Borough, got me relieved from that onerous duty, to run a library van, for St Pancras Borough Council.

The seven years of the war were a prolonged nightmare of uncertainty, inner misery and horror-struck fascination, to see the death of the millions. No one knew when he would be struck dead by the splinter of a bomb, of V1 or V2. We used to meet in Dr Sinha's Indian bookshop and gloat over the defeats of the British, especially when Churchill refused to apply the Atlantic charter of freedom to India.

Jawaharlal Nehru was one of the few Indians, who did not renounce his faith in the struggle against fascist violence, because it was akin to Imperial violence, and yet did not rejoice over the fascist victories.

I also tried to keep a glass wall between Imperialism and Fascism, knowing, the latter would be the end of all human decencies if it won, as it nearly did.

And I joined the war effort, as a casual broadcaster, with George Orwell, the anarchist, in 1942, when Russia was attacked. I have to admit, in retrospect, that I was the victim of the collapse of all morality. The world had reverted back to the cannibalism of the earliest period of man's evolution.

On my return to India in 1946, I saw Faiz in the uniform of the British-Indian army. His collaboration, like mine, may have been the thin veneer of rationalisation, similar to mine. Always the colonisers had left very little choice to the colonised to remain pure. We were all trained with compromises, even though we protested.

But the biggest fall was when we had to accept partition between 'India that is Bharat' and Pakistan.

The bellicose enthusiasms for personal gain of the upper hierarchies, masquerading as religion, inspired the mobs to kill and get killed. There were half a million dead on both sides.

Most of us were numbed by the scare of the murders. To us the warring seventy-two sects of Islam had been perverting religion for generations: equally, the caste oppression of the Hindus was an abomination: so that Gandhiji had equated the struggle against untouchability with struggle for freedom. We were groping towards faith in the growth of men and women, and were apostates.

After some time I tried to write a novel, entitled The Brother, describing the enforced separation of two poets just before the partition riots. It was based on my parting from Faiz and other friends, when Mian Iftikhar-ud-Din motored me from Lahore to Delhi via Bhatinda road at the risk of his life. Our mentor, Jawaharlal Nehru, sent my rescuer back with a guard, asking him to stay put in the new state and work for ultimate amity.

Even these meetings were few and far between. We heard with dismay a few years after the foundation of Pakistan that both Sajjad Zaheer, who had been sent to rally the radicals in Pakistan, and Faiz were accused of participating in the plot to murder the Prime Minster of Pakistan, Liaqat Ali Khan. And they were both detained in a jail in Baluchistan for some years.

The details about the frame-up were given to me by Iftikhar-ud-Din, in 1950, when he came to represent Pakistan in greeting the new Chinese Republic, at the same time as Jawaharlal Nehru sent a delegation from India under Pandit Maulvi Sunderlal, 'an old Gandhian mystic Marxist', as he called himself. I was one of the delegates.

Iftikhar-ud-Din said he had started a paper *The Pakistan Times* and made Faiz the Editor, with Mazhar Ali, descendant of the old feudal family of Sikandar Hayat Khan, as Assistant Editor. But it had already found it difficult to survive, because of its liberal democratic outlook. Ifti had not brought any newly published books, but though not a very keen observer of political trends, he said, most of them were walking in the footsteps of Iqbal, Josh and Faiz, and were protesting as underground 'guerrillas' for egalitarian aims. He himself, was deeply impressed by the land distribution ceremonies we witnessed in villages near Shanghai, and he wished, when he got back, to do what Tolstoy had done-'give away his lands to the peasants'.

I felt that there may be the immanent will of our collective unconscious, emerging to reason and, compelled by love, working in all of us, as our hearts beat in unison.

It was love of people that had made Sajjad Zaheer, son of the Lord Chief Justice of the Oudh High Court, give up everything to become a secretary to Jawaharlal Nehru. The same force had compelled Mahmud-ud-Zaffar, the scion of a Taluqdar family to join the Congress, against his cousin, the Raja of Mahamudabad, who was one of the big ones of the Muslim League. And a similar inspiration had made Dr Muhammad Ashraf give up writing history to join others to make history. And Faiz Ahmed Faiz was driven by the same passion.

Denied pen and paper, during his incarceration, he wrote with coal so that he would make every stone of his jail speak of freedom.

This immanent will to love unto death was the unconscious strain of the moving lines of his later poems.

The expression of love for the beloved in Faiz's poetry is not what it was in the mystics, Rumi, Jami and Nizami. As in Iqbal, it is emergent will, which connects the lover and the beloved, in his case, himself and others. He seems to feel that when God is called Love, the Divine becomes an anti-vital element. Faiz wished to include the magnetism of romantic physical love in his willed extroversion before he could make the symbol of his romantic love of people, come alive. His attitude towards the phenomenal world is passionate, allying the inner stirring of feelings with the rhythms of the universe itself.

Every time we met during a gathering in Delhi, Berlin, Moscow, Tashkent, Helsinki, Havana or London, our meetings were celebrations of love. The poems he recited were full of the longing for those who were separated from him, the old melancholy of Urdu poetry became yearning.

And to him Islam meant what it was supposed to be - the religion of peace. If he could not persuade the egoists around him in the seats of power to relent from making religion the cue for war, he certainly joined others of like mind, outside the prison of his land, to defy the promised death of the nuclear holocaust. He had an unbound, unconcealed disregard for official opinions, judgements of authority and the blind forces of hate, acting against life. He travelled tirelessly to bring the awareness of evil, apprehensive that evil may triumph, but keep alive the fight against nearly impossible odds.

Our last meeting was in London in the Spring of 1984, in the Urdu Markaz, founded by those poets and writers who prefer to live in exile from Pakistan.

> We embraced each other after we were garlanded.
>
> And both of us had tears in our eyes.
>
> And then we smiled.
>
> And held hands.

I do not mourn for Faiz. He gave me a recording of his poems. I hear his voice almost every evening. I want to fill myself with his 'hope in despair', in the midst of near despair before the threats of nuclear war.

Abid Hussain*

Faiz was one of the most powerful literary voices

Faiz was one of the most powerful literary voices of the 20th century. As a poet he could be put in the class of Ghalib and Iqbal. It may be no exaggeration to see Faiz as a true heir to Ghalib.

His poetry distinguishes itself from other lyrics in its ability to lay bare the pain of human conditions through the magic of words, imagery and accent of pathos, without diminishing its resonant expressiveness.

Without side stepping the nuances of thoughts, he had the natural gift to combine syntax with semantics and introduce phrases creating a mix of classic and modern tones in a harmonious rhythm. There is a sense of a modern mind behind conventional niceties of classic poetry. His poetry fuses the two into an inseparable unity.

Faiz was a lover of beauty. For him, beauty was the most valuable thing and the power to express its splendour in words was priceless and inspiring. The lustre of beautiful eyes was the crowning glory for him. Through words he would convey their impact and transform them into imaginative, angelic charm. In his heart of hearts, there was always another , wider world which opened up to bestow upon them, an insatiable delight.

Reticence and good manners never let him transgress into anything sordid or sterile. It is through the detour of his words that he revokes their memories and shares the exuberance of a loving heart, blazing through layers of time to become a delightful vision. In this context, even his prolonged hesitation, unfinished lines, and unsaid thoughts had a charm. "..." became enchanting and meaningful.

---

* Abid Hussain is the Chairman of Faiz Centenary Celebration Committee, India. He is a former Commerce Secretary, Govt. of India, also served as India's Ambassador to United States of America.

Faiz was more than a poet, quite different from the ordinary run of the mill poets of his genre. He was a political crusader. Historical circumstances had made him a militant writer. Though he had joined military service, never did he incorporate himself into a system that was organised to shoot down people fighting for freedom or rip them of their humanism. Militancy takes a different form in poetry than it does in other domains.

Faiz believed that poetry cannot be detached from social reality. Social realism was the bedrock of his sensitive mind. Poetry offered an on-going resistance against tyranny. Art, in his view, provides civilizing refinement to the struggles of life. He propounded the responsibilities of intellectuals and himself assumed moral authority for things done in the cause of freedom and peace. In fact, the essence of his personality was fixed by an ideology which played no negligible role in shaping his self and poetry.

Socialism was close to his heart. For most of the people of his country, the depths of socialism remain unfathomable even when they flounder it. Inwardly he was consumed by fires of insatiable passion for freedom. When the freedom from the Raj was won, for which he had relentlessly struggled and suffered, he celebrated it with a burst of joy. But soon he discovered that the freedom we got was not the right freedom. It turned out to be "the s,sum of human suffering". With anguished pathos, he observes, this is not the day we had longed for:

> This blemished day, and the night eaten morning
> Is it what we waited for?

It casts a garish light upon deliverance from foreign rule but hope was not extinguished. He sets fragments of hope, fixed in a timeless context and awakens a higher sense of patriotism. He transfused its inadequacy with work of artistically conceived brilliant poetry. It became a part of his oeuvre.

Faiz was both a radical and a member of the elite. Though a child of decadent feudal culture, for him, high culture was not exclusively to shore up the interests of the bourgeois, identified with social injustices. He would give equal rights to all, irrespective of the class to which they belong. But he would not let liberal thought suffer a set back or be maimed in the name of ancestral beliefs. He was totally hostile to illiberal thoughts and unhesitantly condemned ways in which beliefs were being propagated. He believed in liberating the latent powers of ordinary people by liberating them from the tyranny of their misguided beliefs and the awe and might of the upper classes.

It was by sheer accident of birth that he was trapped in the decadent feudal culture-a world into which he was born, not unhappily but unknowingly. It had a certain captivating charm to which he submitted, but he could not be attached to feudalism and its long obsession with possession of land and cruelty. Knowledge and experience of its ruthless ways made him stand up against it. Misery is not a turn of phrase or a theme of meditation. It exists, it cries out, in despair. He endeavored to awaken the sleeping conscience of people against it. This hovers over his entire work. His socialistic outlook made him an activist, a militant socialist. He ceaselessly raised his voice to break the feudal order. His poetry gave voice to it. He stoked the imagination of people, to make them aspire for a better world order. He assured them that they are not condemned to be mute. He said "when you speak, the day breaks".

Without getting incorporated into a wave of communal frenzy, which was raging all around him and unsettling relations between the two communities and poisoning young minds, he stood like a rock against communal fury. Without being blind to dualities where BINARY rhythm would stare up in despair, he used poetry to enlarge human values which were getting dissipated. He kindled the light of love on both sides of the border and offered a new drive to strengthen common historical and cultural ties between India and Pakistan. To this day, he remains a strong bridge between the two countries.

No regression or repression could hold him back. He sought deliverance from them through truth, expressed in lyrical form. He strongly believed that ideas gave courage to people. Once they are persuaded of their truths, they become an unstoppable force. For any decline in the intensity of belief leads to a decline in effective activity. He therefore, wanted first to strike away those ideas which were ignoble and sordid, which leave people without power and install in them courageous revolutionary thoughts.

While on one side of his poetry there is the fragrance and splendour of love, on the other, there is the thunder and lightning of revolt. He exhorts his people to rebel against repressive regimes: 'Throw their crowns into dust and push their thrones to oblivion'. He said:

> Fear not, your lips are still free
>
> Your words are still your own
>
> Speak before the body and mind die.
>
> Speak. Truth is not dead.

He was so strong and mighty in launching struggle that no waves of repression could stop his rock-like-determination in this regard. He could not be gagged. He could not be silenced. He said:

> I grieve not that you have robbed me of my pen and paper.
>
> For I have dipped my fingers in the blood of my heart.
>
> I grieve not that you have sealed my lips
>
> for I have put my tongue in each loop of the chain

Faiz had fire in his soul which would suffer if it did not blaze. Its flames leap up, consuming the corpse of dead habits and at the height of the flame, a cry is formed creating words to defy the tyranny of the state.

Faiz died when he had still more to say, but men like Faiz do not die. They remain with us for ever. In the words of Sardar Jafri, it can be said - 'I am an ancient player on the stage of time, deathless I rise each time I die'. Faiz lives on!

Sitaram Yechuri*

Celebrating the Idea of Revolution

Faiz Ahmed Faiz was a committed Marxist, one of the greatest Urdu poets, a journalist, film maker, trade unionist, broadcaster, teacher, translator, Lenin Peace Prize winner. Faiz Ahmed Faiz had also served the British Indian Army, rising to the rank of Lt Colonel. Born in Sialkot, Faiz was educated in Lahore, the city which served as his base, throughout his life. He continued to live there after the unfortunate partition of the sub-continent. The trauma, torture and torment of the partition are deeply reflected in his poetry. His love for the liberation of the people of the sub-continent as a whole, was unquestionable. When Mahatma Gandhi was assassinated, a London newspaper said that he was 'a brave enough man to fly from Lahore to Delhi for Gandhi's funeral, at the height of the Indo-Pakistan hatred'.

His work reflects that his identification with the masses of the poor and exploited, his espousal of the cause of liberation from all forms of oppression and exploitation, was complete. He was an active member of the anti-fascist movement and the struggle for freedom from colonialism led by the Communist Party of undivided India. Along with great stalwarts of his time, he was instrumental in founding the Progressive Writers' Association in 1936, when the Communists also organised the students in the All India Students' Federation and the peasantry in the *Kisan Sabha* in the same year.

The Communist Party had sent Comrade Sajjad Zaheer along with some others to organise the Communist Party in Pakistan. Sajjad Zaheer, also a noted and accomplished intellectual and writer, became the founding general secretary of the Communist Party of Pakistan. However, in 1951,

---

* Sitaram Yechury is a Member of Parliament (Rajya Sabha) and a Member of Politburo, Communist Party of India (Marxist)- CPI (M).

Sajjad Zaheer, Faiz Ahmed Faiz and other leading Communists were imprisoned in solitary confinement under sentences of death in the infamous Rawalpindi conspiracy case. Faiz remained in prison for over four years.

Far from either breaking his spirit or sapping his energy for the cause of the revolution, imprisonment stimulated Faiz's creativity. The remarkable tribute brought out by Pakistan's leading group of newspapers *Dawn*, in 2004, informs us of his impressions during imprisonment. "Like love", he wrote, "imprisonment is a basic experience. It opens many new windows of the soul." Some of his best works were to emerge from the confinements of the jails. 'Dast-e-Saba' (The touch of the Morning Breeze) and 'Zindan Nama' (prison journal) elevated him to the status of a literary poetic genius.

In 'Dast-e-Saba', he reflects the basic essence of the Marxist outlook when he states that: "The understanding of the struggle of human life, and a participation in it is not only a pre-requisite of life, it is also a pre-requisite of art".

While studying the eternal man-nature dialectic, Marx and Engels reached the conclusion that as individuals express their life, so they are, what they are coincides with their production, both with what they produce and how they produce. Hence what individuals are, depends upon material conditions of production.

Eric Hobsbawm, in his latest book 'How to Change the World: Tales of Marx and Marxism' recollects that at the 2007 Jewish book week coinciding with Marx's death anniversary, Jacques Attali while paying tribute to Marx had said, "Philosophers before him had thought of man in his totality, but he was the first to apprehend the world as a whole which is at once political, economic, scientific and philosophical". This personal attribute of Marx is actually a reflection of the attribute of the Marxist world outlook. This goes beyond the conventional meaning of `interdisciplinary' approach to the world. Marxism, a creative science, is trans-disciplinary which integrates all disciplines of thought and creative capacities of the human mind.

Faiz, in a sense, reflects such an integrated approach through his life and work in the times that he lived. In his preface to The Rebel's Silhouette, Agha Shahid Ali says: "Faiz was such a master of the *ghazal*, a form that predates Chaucer, that he transformed its every stock image and, as if by magic, brought absolutely new associations into being. For example, the beloved, an archetypal figure in Urdu poetry, can mean friend, woman, God. (Or, for that matter, Motherland, that Bahadur Shah Zafar, lamented for his burial, when blinded in confinement by the British in Rangoon.) Faiz not only tapped into those meanings, but extended them to include the Revolution. "Waiting for the Revolution can be as intoxicating as waiting for one's lover."

Adopting the pen name, Faiz, which can be best described to mean `dedication to the service of his fellow men', he revolutionised Urdu poetry. He relentlessly showed that the pen is mightier than the sword in rousing the people. Just one example of his work as a poet of the Revolution, is his work known as 'Hum Dekhenge':

> We shall witness,
> It is certain that we shall witness
> The day for which there is a promise,
> The day recorded in the eternal tablet,
> When the weighty mountains of cruelty and oppression,
> Shall be blown about like cotton-wool;
> When under the feet of the oppressed ones
> The earth shall shake noisily,
> And over the heads of despotic rulers
> Thunder claps will burst ...
> When the crowns will be toppled,
> And thrones overturned......

His eternal humanism, which, in the first place, led him to embrace Marxism and its world outlook, drove Faiz to espouse the cause of revolution all across the globe. He was a true internationalist.

In the book 'Poetry East', Carlo Coppola calls him: "A spokesperson for the world's voiceless and suffering people whether it be Indians oppressed by the British in the '40s, freedom fighters in Africa, the Rosenbergs during the Cold War, America in the '50s, Vietnamese peasants fleeing American napalm in the '60s, or Palestinian children living in refugee camps in the 1970s".

Faiz travelled abroad widely, some times out of choice as the Editor of the Afro-Asian literary magazine, Lotus being published from Beirut. On some other occasions, he travelled abroad in exile.

Edward W. Said described a meeting with Faiz: "To see a poet in exile - as opposed to reading the poetry of exile - is to see exile's antimuons embodied and endured. Several years ago, I spent some time with Faiz Ahmed Faiz, the greatest of contemporary Urdu poets. He had been exiled by Zia-ul-Haq's military regime and had found a welcome of sorts in the ruins of Beirut. His closest friends were Palestinians." Further he said in his essay 'The Mind of Winter: Reflections on Life in Exile': "The crucial thing to understand about Faiz is that like Garcia Marquez he was read and listened to, both by the literary elite and by the masses...His purity and precision were astonishing, and you must imagine therefore a poet whose poetry combined the sensuousness of Yeats with the power of Neruda. He was, I think, one of the greatest poets of this century".

Much has been written and will, indeed, be written in the future about the work of this socially committed literary genius and a dedicated Communist. A particular lesson that every one of us, who aspires for and works towards Revolution, must learn, is to combine the passion of commitment with creativity. Faiz did this with his poetry and mastered the use of classical forms, transforming them before his audience rather than break from the old forms. He makes you hear and recite his revolutionary message in the old and the new together and at once.

Rakesh Sood*

Faiz, a poet for all times

Faiz Ahmed Faiz was born a hundred years ago, on 13 February 1911, in a village near Sialkot, a small town in western Punjab; today, part of Pakistan. Sialkot has the distinction of producing the two great poets of Urdu in the 20th century - Allama Mohammed Iqbal born a generation earlier in 1875 known as Pakistan's national poet, and Faiz, who is described as Pakistan's unofficial poet laureate. Faiz lived most of his life in the subcontinent (Amritsar, Lahore and Karachi) though he travelled abroad frequently from the 1950s onwards, and in later years lived in Beirut (1978-82). Faiz wrote in Urdu (and in Punjabi, too), a language spoken in Pakistan and parts of north and central India. It is neither a classical language like Sanskrit or Latin nor a global language like English or French. So what lies behind Faiz's universal appeal? What makes Faiz a poet for all times?

What makes Faiz unique is the distinctive nature of his poetry. He experimented with language and idiom but his experiments were based on solid foundations of classical Urdu poetry over which he enjoyed complete mastery. Urdu may not be a classical language or a global language, but it is a language eminently suited to the *ghazal* and *nazm* genres, particularly in its imagery and romance. Urdu originated a thousand years ago as the lingua franca of 'military camp', from the same Turkish root, which also contributed the word 'horde' to English language. A mixture of Arabic and Persian, used by Central Asian invaders, it took on words from many of the languages, spoken in the North Indian plains but most importantly, it adopted their verb structure and is therefore seen as an Indian language. Urdu poetry combines a sense of harmony coming from its Persian roots along with a sense of simplicity and directness nourished by the dialects of the land in which Urdu blossomed. By the time Faiz started writing, Urdu had developed a rich literary history beginning with Amir Khusro and

* Rakesh Sood is at present, Ambassador of India to France.

including Mohammed Quli Qutubshah, Shamsuddin Wali 'Deccani', Mir Taqi 'Mir', Mirza Rafi 'Sauda', Khwaja Mir 'Dard', Nazir 'Akbarabadi', Sheikh Muhammed Ibrahim 'Zauq', Mirza Asadullah Khan 'Ghalib', Hakim Mohammed Momin Khan 'Momin', Nawab Mirza Khan 'Dagh', Mohammad Iqbal and others.

Faiz's life (1911-1984) spanned over a period of change. Faiz's world was a turbulent one with two World Wars, the depression of the 1930s, the growth of isms-communism and fascism, decolonization and the Middle East conflict. Closer home, Faiz witnessed the independence movement in India, the rise of religious nationalism, India's independence and partition, Pakistan's struggles with military dictatorship and creation of Bangladesh. All these developments impacted Faiz's poetry. His *nazms* reflect political commitment but instead of proselytizing, they expose the inner dilemma and struggle. The humanism comes pouring out. The complexity of the processes is not simplified but respected in its integrity. It is this unmistakable passion which makes Faiz a poet for all times.

Like other Urdu poets, Faiz began with the traditional imagery of the Urdu ghazal - lover (*ashiq*), the beloved (*mashooq*), the rival (*raqeeb*), the wine bearer (*saqi*), the tavern (*maikhana*), the cage (*kafas*), moon (*mehtab*). But by mid-1930s he had started taking on bolder and contemporary themes. He became a communist and remained an unabashed leftist throughout his life. Poetry was his chosen field and his ability to move from poetry of love to poetry of revolution, made him a global poet. His new themes were equally timeless- freedom, dignity, justice. Whatever the theme, Faiz's poetry was always imbued with an extreme musicality.

Faiz's father, Sultan Mohammed Khan was the son of a landless peasant but with the instincts of a wanderer. After studying in the local school in Sialkot, he ran away to Lahore to continue his studies and taught himself Persian and English. A chance encounter with an Afghan nobleman took him to Kabul where he became an important advisor in the courts of Amir Abdul Rehman Khan and then Amir Habibullah. Somewhere, there was a falling out or may be the wanderer's urge overtook him and Sultan Mohammed Khan moved to England where he acquired a law degree at Cambridge and practiced at Lincoln's Inn. In London, he also developed a friendship with Iqbal which was to have a bearing eventually on his son's metier. Returning to Sialkot after many years, he married his last and youngest wife, Fatima, and Faiz was born thereafter.

Faiz's early education was at the Scotch Mission High School under the well known scholar Syed Mir Hasan. Iqbal had studied in the same school till 1893 and like Iqbal, Faiz became one of Mir Hasan's favourite pupils. From Sialkot, Faiz went on to Government College in Lahore in 1929 with a personal recommendation from Allama Iqbal. Languages were his strong suit- Arabic, Persian, Urdu and English. At the *Annual Mushaira* at Government College in 1931, Iqbal was the guest of honour when Faiz's poem was awarded the first prize. By this time, his reputation as a poet had started growing though his themes were the traditional pre-occupations of love, beauty, sorrow, loss, etc. The global Faiz was to emerge later as the journeys of the discovery of the mind began. By 1934, he had obtained a B.A. and an M.A. in Arabic as well as an M.A. in English. His familiarity with the poetry of Keats and Shelley led him to experiment with different forms in Urdu poetry and even in his free verse, there lurks a discipline, underlined by alliterations and its resonances, so unique to Urdu poetry.

Faiz's first job was as an English lecturer in 1935, at the Mohammedan Anglo Oriental College in Amritsar. These were difficult times. The great depression in USA had an impact on the rest of the world. The Ottoman Empire had been divided, the Turkish Caliphate abolished. Faiz's father had died three years ago leaving behind family debts. Faiz's first published work 'Naqsh-e-Fariyadi' (1943) contains many of his poems from this period. The first section of his collection is devoted to what Faiz called the emotional pre-occupation of adolescence and youth, love or more often, unrequited love. But even here we see the tenderness of his language. 'Naqsh-e-Fariyadi' opens with following lines which were penned in 1929:

Last night your lost memory so came into the heart

As spring comes in the wilderness quietly,

As the zephyr moves slowly in deserts,

As rest comes without cause to a sick man

Faiz spent five years in Amritsar and became part of a distinguished literary and intellectual circle. A new movement in art and literature had begun with the setting up of the Progressive Writers' Association (PWA). This group included the Principal of the College where Faiz taught, Sahibzada Mahmood-uz-Zafar and his wife, Dr. Rashid Jahan, Sajjad Zaheer and Ahmed Ali. These four had published a collection of Urdu short stories, *Angaarey*, which created a stir because of its strong critique of traditional practices and was banned by the British government. Sajjad Zaheer became Faiz's friend and remained so till his death in 1973. Faiz mourned him with a tribute:

We shall not now, again visit the flowers
Nor walk together to the martyrs field
Nor talk endlessly of all our lovers
From our bleeding hearts removing the shield

The PWA became a movement attracting some of the best literary and poetic talents of that time including Sibte Hasan, Upendra Nath 'Ashq', Sahir Ludhianavi, Ismat Chugtai, etc. The PWA wanted to bring art and literature closer to the people and also make it more relevant to their day to day existence. The artist and the poet had a social responsibility to expose the ills of society and to present a vision of a more equal and just world. These were heady times indeed for young Faiz and marks the shift in his poetry from *gham-e-jana to gham-e-dauran*, from the sorrows of life and longing to the sorrows of the world and the times. The second section of 'Naqsh-e-Fariyadi' reflects this change with one of Faiz's best known *nazms* 'Mujhse Pehli Si Mohabbat Mere Mehboob Na Maang'. The love for the beloved was no longer enough, there was now a greater pain which could only be addressed by a greater love. The poem ends:

There are other sufferings of the time (world) besides love,
There are other pleasures besides the pleasures of union;
Do not ask from me, my beloved, love like that former one

Like many progressive Muslims of that period, Faiz had been inspired by the Khilafat Movement. It had marked a coming together of Hindu and Muslim communities. But the hopes it generated were quickly dashed by a new wave of oppression. The call for complete independence (*Purna Swaraj*) had been raised; witness Faiz's exasperation and anger resulting in his call to speak, to shout. *Bol* (Speak) is certainly the precursor to the howl of rage of the 1960s:

Speak, your lips are free.
Speak, it is your own tongue.
Speak, it is your own body.
Speak, your life is still yours.

Speak, this brief hour is long enough
Before the death of body and tongue:
Speak, 'cause the truth is not dead yet,
Speak, speak, whatever you must speak.

While in Amritsar, Faiz met his future wife, Alys. Alys was a member of the British Communist Party. She was visiting India to meet her elder sister Christabel who was married to Dr. Mohammed-din-Taseer, Faiz's colleague at the Mohammedan Anglo Oriental College and a founding member of PWA. Before coming to India, Alys had been a supporter of India's independence movement, having worked as V.K. Krishna Menon's secretary in London. Faiz and Alys were inspired by similar ideals of freedom, justice and humanity. The marriage took place at Dr. Taseer's house in Srinagar in 1941 with Sheikh Abdullah *performing the Nikaah.* In attendance were many of the progressive poets and writers, a group that increasingly became Faiz's extended family and continued to claim his affection in both India and Pakistan, after partition.

World War II had become a struggle between democracy and fascism and also between communism and fascism. Faiz joined the struggle, to work in the propaganda department of the British Army. He held the rank of a Lieutenant Colonel and was honoured with an MBE, when he took off his uniform in 1947. Independence was the realisation of a dream but how coloured it was with the tragedy and sorrow of partition! Nobody (other than the memorable film 'Garam Hawa' by MS Sathyu, decades later) captures the sadness like Faiz did in August 1947:

> This mottled daybreak, this night-bitten dawn,
>
> This is not that long awaited dawn;

Faiz had seen the tragedy of partition. A million people killed, more than ten million rendered homeless, and months later, the first war between India and Pakistan. Faiz chose Pakistan because he believed in Jinnah's ideas of a secular Pakistan and Sialkot, his place of birth was in Pakistan. But soon thereafter, Faiz was to become disenchanted with the direction of political developments. Just before independence, Faiz had taken over as the Editor of a new English daily newspaper *The Pakistan Times,* which had been started by Mian Iftikharuddin. Mian Iftikharuddin came from a well known family in Punjab and had been a senior member of the Indian National Congress, switching to the Muslim League in 1946, when it was becoming clear that partition was inevitable. Poetry took a back seat and Faiz now started writing hard hitting editorials and prose. Faiz's prose had passion but lacked the elegance of his poetry and was often ponderous. Perhaps, Urdu is a language more suited to poetry than prose; the optimism of a 'secular Pakistan' dreamt of by its founder Mohammad Ali Jinnah soon began evaporating. Jinnah died in 1948 of tuberculosis; in 1951 Liaqat Ali Khan was assassinated and early 1950s saw heated debates in Pakistan Constituent Assembly about the role of Islam in Faiz's homeland. By 1950, Faiz's disenchantment with his country's political leadership was already visible in his editorials.

He was not alone in his disenchantment. A group of Pakistani military officers led by Major General Akbar Khan, were also equally disappointed. Faiz had known Major General Akbar Khan during his stint with the British Army. Faiz arranged a meeting between the General and his old friend Sajjad Zaheer who headed the Communist Party of Pakistan. Not much came out of the meeting but in 1951, some of the individuals involved were exposed, along with their grandiose plans of a military revolution (inspired by Kamal Attaturk in Turkey) to bring about a progressive state.

The Rawalpindi conspiracy as it was called, shook the Pakistani establishment. Faiz spent four years in jail. It was a difficult time but in terms of poetry, the most productive. Two more volumes emerged from his years of incarceration - 'Dast-e-Saba' in 1953 and 'Zindan Nama' in 1956. By this time, Faiz's fame had spread beyond Pakistan's borders. He had defined his role as a poet - it was no longer limited to perception and observation of the environment; a poet's role was also to set in motion, the processes of change which implied a struggle. Faiz, the perennial rebel had come of age.

In years that followed, Faiz's image as a revolutionary poet, crossed the oceans and continents. In March 1955, Faiz wrote 'Aa Jao Africa':

> Come, I have heard the ecstasy of your drum
>
> Come, the beating of my blood has become mad
>
> Come, Africa! ...
>
> I am Africa, I have taken your figure,
>
> I am you, my walk is your lion walk:
>
> Come, Africa!

After his release, Faiz travelled abroad, building friendships and new relationships. He translated the Turkish poet Nazim Hikmet (1902-1983) into Urdu. Hikmet was then described as a romantic communist. Faiz developed a special relationship with Chilean poet Pablo Neruda (1904-1973) who was also a fellow traveller. Aime Cesaire (1913-2008), the poet, politician and activist from Martinique and Langston Hughes (1902-1967) an American black poet who was among the pioneers of the Harlem Renaissance, provided Faiz with an insight into the issues of negritude. Faiz's internationalism paralleled the growth of third worldism reflected in the beginning of the Non-Aligned Movement. The Cold War had cast its shadow and it is quite clear which side Faiz was on. In his own country, there was a perceptible shift in the other direction, as Pakistan got drawn closer to the Western bloc, becoming a member of SEATO and CENTO, both US-led military alliances. When Ethel and Julius Rosenberg were executed in the US for being communist spies, their letters inspired Faiz to write:

> Picking up our flags from these grounds
> Will march forth more caravans of your lovers
> For whose journeys' sake, our footsteps
> Have shortened the lengths of the agonizing quest
> For whose sake we have made universal
> by losing our lives, the pledge to your faithfulness
> We, who were slain in unlit pathways.

By 1958, Pakistan was under its first spell of military rule. President Iskander Mirza had taken General Ayub Khan's support to declare martial law only to find that he soon had to yield to General Khan, who became the Chief Martial Law Administrator and then President of Pakistan. Faiz had several brushes with the establishment during this period including another stint in jail for six months. However, his international fame kept growing and to some extent also protected him. In 1962, Faiz was awarded the Lenin Peace Prize, which the Soviet Union had launched as the equivalent of the Nobel Prize. This made Faiz especially well known in the Eastern bloc and he was widely translated into all the Soviet bloc languages including Czech, Polish, etc. During this period, Faiz developed his strong support for the Palestinian cause, something that would take him to Beirut, years later, when Pakistan was under yet another spell of military rule, under General Zia-ul-Haq.

Faiz was troubled by the deterioration in relations between India and Pakistan, the two countries where he enjoyed total adulation and cult status. In 1965, instead of writing stirring patriotic songs for Pakistan, Faiz wrote 'Sipahi ka Marsiya':

> Rise now from the dust
> My darling young one. Wake.
> Wake now. Wake now.
> We've your life's bed to make.

Look how the dark night
Comes wrapped in a long blue shawl
Where these crying eyes
Have heaped up pearls

The next blow was the creation of Bangladesh. After the 1965 India-Pakistan war, General Ayub Khan tried to sell the Tashkent Agreement at home, but the Muslim parties accused him of betraying the Kashmiri cause. His Foreign Minister Zulfiqar Ali Bhutto distanced himself and in 1969, President Ayub was succeeded by General Yahya Khan. The promised elections yielded an outcome in favour of the Awami League even though Pakistani provinces had been made into a single unit. East Pakistan came under brutal repression. Martial law was imposed. Poets, academics and intellectuals in Dhaka were rounded up and many were slaughtered. After Bangladesh came into being, General Yahya Khan was discredited and a new civilian government took over, in Pakistan. There was hope for a return to democracy. Prime Minister Zulfiqar Ali Bhutto offered the post of Cultural Advisor to Faiz Ahmed Faiz. Faiz's lasting contributions during his five years in the government, was the creation of the Pakistan National Council of Arts and the Lok Virsa (an organisation set up to preserve folk traditions and heritage). Faiz's silence, during the genocide in East Pakistan, is something that has always puzzled and intrigued his admirers. He accompanied Prime Minister Bhutto to Bangladesh in 1974. On his return, as if in expiation he wrote 'Dhaka se Vapsi Par':

How I wanted, but how my fractured heart did not allow
Flirtatious complaints after the supplications were over

And what you came so willing to give up all for, Faiz
Was utterly unvoiced when all the talking was over

Pakistan's period of democracy was to prove short lived. Bhutto resorted to populism and started flirting with the Islamic parties. Islam was declared the State religion, making minorities, second class citizens. When Bhutto conceived of Pakistan's nuclear bomb, he sold the idea to the oil rich Arab countries as an 'Islamic bomb'. Amidst allegations of election rigging in which the Islamic parties opposed Bhutto, democracy ended and General Zia-ul-Haq took over in 1977. Faiz realized with a heavy heart, that the time had come to leave. He went first to Delhi, where he was offered a Chair by a number of universities. Some of his Pakistani friends felt that this might be politically incorrect. Faiz then left for Moscow and spent time there as well as in London. In London he wrote 'Dil-e-Man Musafir-e-Man':

My heart, my fellow traveler
It has been decreed again
That you and I be exiled

During his travels, Faiz had developed and enjoyed a close relationship with the Afro-Asian Writers Association and was appointed Editor of the Association's journal, *Lotus*. Beirut was the location which suited Faiz perfectly. Faiz had a strong sympathy for the Palestinian cause and Beirut then was also Yassir Arafat's base. A lot of his poetry of that period reflects his travails and the pain of the Palestinian people. Among the most moving, is his "Lullaby for a Palestinian Baby":

Child, don't cry
Your mother has just slept, weeping=
Child, don't cry
A little while ago,
Your father has bid farewell to his sorrows ...
Child, don't cry
If you cry then mother, father,
elder sister, brother, moon and sun
Will give you cause to cry more
If you smile, then may be,
All of them, in different guises,
Will return to play with you.

In 1982, when Israel attacked Lebanon, Beirut became a battlefield and Faiz came to Moscow. His health had deteriorated and he missed his homeland. His friends assured him that President Zia-ul-Haq would not pose obstacles to his return. So Faiz ended his self exile and returned to Lahore in 1983. He died a year later, on 20 November 1984. Faiz's *takhallus* reveals the man - liberalism, grace and a desire to share. Faiz's poetry reflects all three. In 1979, Faiz composed one of his memorable nazms 'Hum Dekhenge' which became the rallying cry against Zia-ul-Haq's military rule:

We shall see
With certainty, we too, shall see ....

When these mountains heavy
With tyranny and oppression
Will fly away like wraps of cotton in the air

And we oppressed
Beneath our feet will feel
this earth's shuddering beat
And heads of rulers
Will be struck
With crackling lightning...

Then the masses, God's own, will rule
Which I am too
and so are you

In Pakistan, this was also the rallying cry when General Pervez Musharraf tried to muzzle the judiciary, which would have pleased Faiz to no end. It could also have been the rallying cry in Tahrir Square or the Pearl Square ... indeed anywhere or everywhere, wherever a hopeful human being raises his head against tyranny.

Faiz speaks

Faiz Ahmed Faiz

About myself and what I have been up to ...

On 7 March 1984, just eight months before he died, Faiz Ahmed Faiz was invited to talk to the Asia Study Group in Islamabad. This slightly edited version of the transcript - he spoke extempore - was published for the first time by ***Pakistan Times*** *on the occasion of his birth anniversary on 13 February, 1990 - Editor.*

Thank you very much for inviting me over. I asked Pasha what he wanted me to talk about. He said, 'about yourself and what you have been up to'. In a way, that came as a relief, which means I did not have to prepare a discourse. At the same time, I found it disconcerting for two reasons: firstly, because it is quite some years since I arrived at the age of what Disraeli calls, 'the age of anecdotes' and secondly, because I have been, for such a long time, in an unconscious frame of mind, that I would not know, how to cut a long story, short.

I was born in the house of a gentleman, who was a nineteenth century adventurer, who had a far more colourful life than I have had. He was born in the house of a landless peasant in a small village, in our Sialkot district. And, according to the story he told us, (which of course had been authenticated by other members of the village) because his father was a landless peasant, he was employed by the people, who had some land to tend to their cattle. So he said, 'I used to take the cattle out of the village, and I found that there was a school, a little distance away from the village. I would leave the cattle to graze and attend the school'. Thus, he passed his primary. Then he said 'there was no further education in my village, so I ran away to Lahore'. There he lived in a mosque and he said 'in the evening I used to go to the railway station and work as a coolie. During the day, I would study. And every mosque in our days (unfortunately, it is one of the customs which has died out) served as a house for indigent students, and food was provided by people of the area, and education was provided by the priest in the mosque itself or somebody, and these students got free education.'

When he was living in this mosque, it so happened that an Afghan grandee was counsel to the Government of the Punjab. He used to come and pray in this mosque. He saw this young boy and he rather liked him and he said 'Look, we want an English interpreter for Afghanistan'. This was the time of the grandfather of the ruler of Afghanistan, before Nadir Shah, because after every one, two or three years, one dynasty was overthrown and another dynasty came into power. The dynasty which was overthrown in 1924-25 was that of Amanullah Khan; his grandfather was the king at that time. Anyway, this King wanted an English interpreter because this was the time when the Durand Treaty was being negotiated between the British and the Afghans. So this Afghan diplomat said, "Would you like to go to Afghanistan?" My father said, "Why not. I have nothing else to do". The king employed him, firstly as interpreter and then he negotiated with the British. Later on, he became his chief secretary, then his minister, and so on and so forth. There were a number of tribes which were conquered during his period and every time a tribe's area was taken, the princesses of the vanquished tribe were distributed among the courtiers. So my father got his share of my stepmothers (I don't know how many - three or four).

Anyway, after spending about fifteen years in the service of the king, he got fed up because he was an outsider and naturally all the ministers and grandees of the court were feudal. So they got resentful of this man, encroaching on their preserve. He said that he was often denounced as a British spy and every time he was sentenced to death, it was discovered that the charge was false and then he got a promotion. So he thought, 'one day they might carry it (death sentence) out'. Thus, he disguised himself as a beggar and escaped, came to Lahore and was promptly arrested there as an Afghan spy!

There was an English woman, an adventurer like him, who had descended on the court as a doctor. Her name was Dr. Hamilton and they became friends. The various bounties that he got from the king, this woman was wise enough to take a part of it and invest it in London. So when he was thrown out, she wrote to him from England and said, 'Come to London'. He went to London and joined Cambridge University as a student. The Afghan king, seeing that he had escaped, said, "Well, since you are in London, why don't you become my ambassador?" Later on he joined the Bar and got his law degree, and at the same time continued to be an ambassador. In Persian there is a saying, if anyone wants to boast about his father, he says 'my father was king', the word for king being, 'Sultan'. Now my father's name was Sultan, so I can say my father was Sultan!

Anyway, after getting his law degree, instead of going back to Afghanistan, he landed up in his own town, or rather his own district, which is Sialkot. And when the king found out that he had left, he sent his family to Sialkot-my stepsisters and maybe also a stepmother or two. Now there is a novel about him called 'Daughter ...' something. It is out of print, but perhaps you can find it in some old library, written by this English woman. So, he came back and started law practice. Once my stepmother died, he married my mother from the next village. My mother and stepsisters were thus, more or less of the same age; the elder sister was older than she was.

We went to school in Sialkot; I got my first schooling in the mosque, a mosque in our locality. There were two schools in the town, one belonged to the Scotch Mission, and the other belonged to the American Mission. I went to the Scotch Mission because it was near the house. Later on, the American mission packed up. This period - the end of the First World War and the beginning of the 1920s - was a period of great upheaval in India. There were various nationalist movements belonging to all the three communities. The Congress movement had both Hindus and Muslims in its leadership, but the rank and file were largely Hindus. There was the Khilafat Movement of the Muslims, the Muslims being romantic people. This was the time after the First World War and the Turks had been defeated and the Ottoman Empire was disintegrating and the Turks were fighting against, both the British and the Greek invaders. The Muslims of India, started a movement to save the Caliph, whom they had never seen, never known and who was somewhere in Turkey. They could not save him because he was thrown out by Kamal Ataturk, the founder of modern Turkey. The Sikhs started the Akali movement to assume the caretakership of the Sikh shrines. So all the three, the Muslims, the Hindus, and the Sikhs, for a short period of about 6-7 years, made common cause against the British and there was great upheaval, all over the country. In our small town of Sialkot, great leaders like Mahatma Gandhi and Nehru's father and the leaders of the Sikhs, visited; whenever they came to the town, the whole city was decorated, flower gates were set up and the whole city turned out to welcome them. That is how one imbibed; one got the first whiff of politics during those very eventful years.

At the same time, the October Revolution had taken place. News of that event also filtered down into Sialkot. I heard people talking, 'Look, we have heard that in this country called Russia, somebody called Lenin has overthrown the king and he has distributed the wealth of all the people among the workers. Suppose you rob a banker and distribute his wealth, it would be great fun!'

Anyway, that was what was going on in our early schooldays. In school, I got inducted into poetry, in two ways. Firstly, next to our house, was a small bookshop, run by a young man, who lent books-rented them out at 2 paise a book, a week. So I borrowed all the books that he had. All my pocket money was spent on reading these books. I had read all the classics by the time I got into high school. Secondly, in this town, there was already great name for the great Poet; Iqbal was born in the same town and therefore his poems were recited and sung in the common current. And, thirdly, a big mansion next to our house, which during the day was a primary school where I studied, in the evenings, once a month, became the venue for what we call a *mushaira*. When I was in my last year of school, our headmaster said, "Look, I am going to have a competition. I will compose five or six couplets from this line and we will send these couplets to the great scholar of the town (who was a teacher of the great poet Iqbal) and he will decide who wins the prize." I won the prize. The prize was one rupee, which was a fortune in those days.

After finishing my two years at Sialkot, I went to Lahore, to Government College. Now, coming from a small town like Sialkot into Lahore, was just like coming to a foreign country. Because at that time there was no running water in the town (Sialkot), there was no electricity.

Water was brought to the house by water carriers or if they did not come, you had to fetch water from the well. Every locality had its own well, and some of the big houses had their own wells. There was no electricity; we read by kerosene oil lamps which are very interesting, very picturesque lamps. There were no cars in Sialkot. Even the head of the district, the Deputy Commissioner, used to come in a horse driven carriage. He had a one-horse carriage while my father had a two-horse carriage.

Anyway, I came to Lahore; here for the first time we saw cars and we saw people in those wonderful dresses and we saw young women, going about without veils. And in this college, half the teachers were English, unlike our college in Sialkot, and everything was out of this world. My English teacher was an old man called Langhorn, extremely bad-tempered, but a very good teacher. At the very first examination that I took in college, in my first English paper I got 63 marks out of 150. So, everybody hung their heads and I immediately became a celebrity. The senior scholars, the Muslim scholars, who later on became high civil officials in Pakistan, said, “Look, start preparing for the Indian Civil Service examination.” I said, "All right". But at that time, instead of preparing for the Indian Civil Service examination, I started gradually becoming a poet. Two or three things determined that. First of all, the trial; before I finished my first degree, my father died and I suddenly discovered that from being grandees and rich men of the town, we became paupers. He had left some property-some landed property-but he had left bigger debts than the property. That was one factor that had great impact on my family and myself. Secondly, suddenly came the Great Depression. As a result, the prices of agricultural produce went below rock bottom. The countryside became very impoverished and the little income that we had left, from land, also stopped. The Great Depression had a great impact, politically and personally, not only on myself, but also on whole communities, particularly of the Muslims. They were mainly an agricultural community and they depended entirely for a living, on what the land brought and the land brought hardly anything. So there was no employment because there were hardly any industries. Whatever industries were there, belonged to non-Muslims.

The third avenue of employment was Government service. And there again, the Muslims, who were educationally backward, could not really find jobs. So, politically and personally, this was a period of great hardship for the family. On top of it all, there was one thing which created the impulse and the motivation for expressing this ordeal into poetry; I fell in love as everybody does at that age of 17 or 18. I fell in love with an old playmate of mine, an Afghan girl, whose family had come from Afghanistan at the same time as my father. When we were children, their family left Sialkot and she went into purdah (seclusion) when she was 12 or 13 and I had not seen her since childhood. They settled in a village near what I know as Faisalabad and my sister was married in that town. So I went to this village to see this family and there, one morning, I woke up and saw a very beautiful girl, feeding a parrot. She looked at me and I looked at her and then we promptly fell in love; rather, I did. As was the custom, we, sort of secretly, held hands, but that's as far as we could go. But the next day, she was married off to some rich landlord. She went there the first time as a girl. When she came back, I never met her again. So we lived unhappily ever afterwards- for eight years. By this time, I was concentrating on my education and I think after reciting at my third mushayra, I was acknowledged as a writer or as a poet. Then, in the town of Lahore, the great writers, my senior writers who were my teachers, well, they adopted me, as one of their proteges, and so I became a poet.

This was the period of the first terrorist movement in the subcontinent. These terrorists had also infiltrated our college and one of the members was a bosom pal of mine, who later on became a great music composer, Khwaja Khurshid Anwar. He was arrested while stealing acid from the college laboratory to make a bomb and was sentenced for three years time, some of which he served. Then, they let him go because his father was an influential man. I got to know things through him, he used to leave his illegal literature in my room in the hostel. Sometimes, when I flipped through it, I felt very frightened, because my father was a titled person, acknowledged as one of the well wishers of the British Empire. That is how I got to know terrorism and some of the phraseology of revolutionaries. That must have rubbed off on me, but I did not take much notice of it.

After three or four years, I finished my degree. I first got a Master's degree in English, then I got a degree in Arabic and then I started teaching and that was the time when I got over this period of great hardship and my brother got a job and the family was slightly better off.

During this period, my colleagues in college, two people who had come back from Oxford had become Marxists, and they introduced me to Marxism. Later on, a whole bunch of young men, returned from British universities - all belonging to rich or aristocratic families and all communists. Some of them stayed communist, others, after dabbling in it for a few years, took on various jobs. Anyway, they came back and they started a literary movement which was called the Progressive Writers' Movement. It was not a communist or a Marxist movement as such; although many of the office holders belonged to this group, it was a realistic sort of movement. Because previously during the classical period and the periods afterwards, our poetry and our literature was very largely given to legends and fanciful tales and romanticizing and poetry was largely, linguistic gymnastics. During this period, a genuine, lyrical, political poetry was born.

At the same time during the 1930s, the great anti-fascist movement rose and the literary movements, both in Europe and in America turned to literature of social comment. We got directly influenced by the movement and that is how between 1932 and 1935, I got involved in this political-cum-literary movement. Secondly, in trade unions and workers' or peasants' movements and thirdly, by creating a new style that was an amalgam both of lyricism and of politics, of classicism and modernism and that appealed to the people. When my first book came out in 1941, it was an immediate best-seller. Then came the war. First of all, we did not care much about the war. We thought this was something concerned with the British and the Germans, but in 1941, the Japanese entered the war. On the one hand, the Japanese came to the borders of India and on the other hand, the Nazis and the Fascists, came to the doorsteps of Moscow and Leningrad. We felt that it was time to go and join the fight, so we joined the army. I joined the army and I remember my first day when I was produced before the Public Relations Department Officer. He was not a regular soldier; he was really a journalist from the London Times, a very jovial Irishman. He said, "Look, I have your police report. It says you are an advanced communist. Are you?" I said, "I don't know what a retarded communist is." So he said, "I do not care, you may even be a Fascist, so long as you do not let us down. You won't let us down?" I said, "No".

This was the time when on the one hand, the British and the Allies were not having a good time during the war. On the other hand, Mahatma Gandhi had started his 'Quit India' Movement and that movement spread like wildfire. So, the British had two problems on their hands: recruiting people for the Army and at the same time, fighting this great movement against the British Raj. The brigadier started talking to me about this movement. He said, "What line do we take on this movement so far as the Indian troops are concerned?" I said, "We take no line at all." He said, "What do you mean?" I said, "What I mean is, the line you take is, you are not fighting for the British, you are not fighting for what we call the salt, but you're fighting for your country, because now your country is in danger, because the Japanese are on the brink and the British will walk out after two to three years because they've been fighting here for so long. If the Japanese or the Germans come, that means you will be slaves for a hundred or two hundred years. So we have to defend our land - you are not fighting for the British, you're fighting for India".

He said, “My boy, but that's politics, how do we make it acceptable to the army? How do I put it across to the army?" I said, “Put it across the same way the communists do". He said, “What do you mean” I said, "We make a cell, a proper kind of cell in every unit of the army and through this cell we teach, first the officers, as to what is Fascism, what the Japanese are doing, what the Italians are doing. Then we ask them. Because our soldiers are not very literate, so you can only teach them by word of mouth. So first we will teach the teachers, we will teach them about Fascism, the Japanese, etc., etc., then they will teach the men and we will form these groups." After a great deal of controversy, it went to the Viceroy, it went to the Commander-in-Chief, and it went to the India Office. He said, "Write it down". I wrote down the scheme. Finally, it was approved. We started these groups; they were called *Josh Groups. Josh* means fervour, enthusiasm, and èlan. So these groups were formed. They were very successful and that is how I got my order of the British Empire.

And through various ways, I became a colonel in three years. This was the highest rank you could attain as an Indian at that time. During this period, firstly, I came to know the army; secondly, I came to know the British; and thirdly, I could not write much poetry but I learned journalism, because I was in charge of the entire publicity for the entire Indian Army on all the fronts and I became, more or less, the political Commissioner of the Indian Army. The war ended, and then I left the army and I had the option of either going into the Foreign Service or into the Civil Service. "Well", I said, "nothing doing".

That was a time when the movement for Pakistan and the movement of the Indian Congress, were at their height. An old friend of mine - a big landlord - who was previously, the president of the Punjab Congress party, moved over to the Muslim League and he said, 'Look, to hell with Foreign Service and Civil Service, we want to start a daily in Lahore. You come and edit this paper'. So in January 1947, I came to Lahore and started *The Pakistan Times*. I edited it for four years. At the same time I became vice president of the Pakistan Trade Union. At the same time in 1948, after Hiroshima and Nagasaki, the Korean War started. We got an appeal from Stockholm that we should start a peace movement. So we made a peace committee. I was in charge of Trade Unions; I was in charge of *The Pakistan Times*. Those were very, very satisfying days, for four years. This is when I first went to Europe, as a workers' delegate to the International Labour Organisation. I attended their meetings, first in San Francisco and then twice in Geneva. This was the first time I was introduced to America and Europe.

From 'Pindi Conspiracy' to Beirut

Then, at the end of 1950, I met an old friend of mine, from the army, who had been appointed Chief of General Staff, General Akbar Khan. He had distinguished himself as a soldier in Burma and then, during the fighting in Kashmir. I met him by chance in Murree, where I was holidaying for ten days and he said to me, "Look, we people in the army, particularly we who fought in Kashmir, are very disgruntled because this country is going to the dogs. We have made no constitution for four years, there is so much corruption, there is so much nepotism, no elections are being held ... and there is no hope and we want to do something." I said, "Do what?" He said, "Overthrow the government and we want to have a non-party government and have elections and a constitution..." and this, that and the other. I said, "All right!" He said, "Well, we want your advice." I said, "Well, this is an army exercise, I can't give you any advice.' He said, "Anyway, you come to our meeting and listen to my plan."

Then, in a very stupid way, I went to his meeting, along with two civilian friends and we listened to this plan. The plan was to occupy the Presidential House, occupy the radio station-of course, there was no TV then-and make the President announce that the government was overthrown and a non-party government had been formed and a new constitution would be promulgated in six months and new elections would be held and then there were to be social reforms, etc. This was discussed for about five or six hours and eventually, - there were about fourteen or sixteen officers there - they decided, after a good deal of discussion, that it was not going to work, for the simple reason, that there was no issue before the country on which you could mobilize the people and, secondly, the thing might have gotten discovered before it went off! Besides, it was too risky. So it was decided that nothing should be done.

However, somebody got cold feet - this was the first Pakistani government under the Prime Ministership of Liaquat Ali Khan. They got really jittery and by this time, I had forgotten all about it. Nothing had happened, you see, nothing was going to be done. Suddenly, one fine morning at about four o'clock, I found my house surrounded by soldiers. Somebody came up and said, "Come along." I said, "What has happened?" He said, 'You are under arrest.'' I said, "What for?" He said, "I do not know what for, but this comes from the Governor-General himself." I said, "We have not done any thing, we do not know what it is all about." For four months, I was put in solitary confinement; I did not know what had happened until after four months. A special Act was passed by the Constituent Assembly; it was called the Rawalpindi Conspiracy Act. Then we were brought to trial, a secret trial under this Act, which was passed only for this particular case.

The conspiracy law from the British days was bad enough, you did not have to do anything, if it was proved that two people had agreed to break the law, it became a conspiracy, and if a third person deposed that he had witnessed these two people agreeing, that was enough. No power to act was necessary; this was all that was necessary under the British law. The government thought that this was not good enough, so they made a special Act abolishing whatever safeguards were open to the Defence, and in this Act, there was really no escape from conviction. It was a long trial, lasting for about a year and a half. Finally, we were all sentenced to various terms of imprisonment according to rank: the general got eight years, the brigadier got seven years, a colonel got six years. We, as civilians, had the lowest sentences - we got four years.

This was the period of my imprisonment which was in some ways, very productive because I had no amusements, I had plenty of time to read and one felt angry all the time, because one knew one was innocent. So during these four years, I wrote two books of poetry. My first book had come out in 1941 and was sold out immediately. These two books came out - one while I was still in prison, the second, when I came out of prison. When you have been in prison for four years and you have been in solitary confinement, it naturally adds to your market value, a great deal. So when I came out, I found myself an even greater celebrity than before. I went back to my newspapers; for another three or four years, I worked for the same papers and continued with the Peace Movement. The trade union movement in the meantime had been destroyed because all the Left organisations had been banned. This lasted for three to four years, and then came the first Martial Law and the first Army government and that was the first march to prison, without any charge. The funny thing was that the government at that time - the Martial Law Government - rounded up everyone, whose names appeared on police files from 1920 onwards!

So, in the prison we found people, ninety years old, eighty years old, many of them were off their nuts, some had died of tuberculosis or something. After four or five months, we were assigned a wonderful judge -everyone who applied for 'habeas corpus' was let out. This was the time when I spent a month and a half in the Lahore Fort, the famous urban concentration place. After four or five months, I was released. So I thought that I would go back to my newspapers. Three days after I was released, I went to my office and found the place surrounded with police. I said,

"What happened?" They said, "It has been taken over." All these newspapers had been confiscated, they had all been taken over by the Military government and that was the end of my journalism career. I said, "What do I do now?" After a short period, since I had friends in high places, because of poetry, they said 'What about doing some culture?' I said 'Very good'. So I founded the Arts Council in Lahore, and even this was in a broken down old building, not the very impressive thing that you see today; the place caught on - exhibitions and concerts and plays, and so on and so forth.

We had funds for three or four years. I fell sick after three or four years of running this place. I had my first heart attack, and during my heart attack, I got the news that I had been given the International Lenin Prize. Somebody called me from the newspaper office 'You have been given the Lenin Prize. I said 'Shut up!' Then I said, "Look, I am sick and you are joking." He said, "No, no, this is no joke, it is on our teleprinter. It said you and Picasso and this, that and the other person."

So when I got over my sickness, I was invited to Moscow to get my prize and also to get my treatment. From Moscow, I went to London, spent two years there and came back. Instead of coming to Lahore, we stayed in Karachi for eight years, because the Haroon family, (your present Minister of the Interior Mahmood Haroon's family) knew me. His sister was a friend of mine, who was a doctor and she said 'Look, we have a charitable Foundation. There is a school, there is a hospital, there is an orphanage and if you have nothing better to do, why don't you take over the Foundation and administer the funds? My sons have no time, they are busy in their business and their politics.' I went and looked at the place. It was right in the slums and this was the centre of the drug peddlers, the camel drivers, the fishermen, and cut-throats. I said 'Very nice, very picturesque.' We made the school into a college, we set up a technical institute, we had a public hall, and we organised the orphanage.

So, for eight years I returned to teaching and administration and then came back. In between there were two wars, the 1965 war with India and the 1971 war in Bangladesh. These two were difficult periods for me because I was under a great deal of pressure to write war songs, but I said 'Look here, I am not writing any war songs!' They said 'Well, why not? It is your patriotic duty. I said 'Look, firstly, because I consider these wars to be a very wanton waste of precious lives and secondly, because I know that Pakistan is not going to get anything out of either this war or that war, I am not going to write any war songs.' But, eventually, I did write poems about both wars. In the first war, I wrote two poems, one was called 'Blackout' and the theme was that it was autumn with the lights - physical lights - which having gone out, symbolised the light of reason gone out, the light of love had gone out, and all the lights in the hearts of people had gone out. And the second poem was an elegy for a fallen soldier and his mother, mourning for her son. This infuriated my patriotic friends even more.

During the second war in Bangladesh, I wrote more than three or four poems. One was 'The Festival of Bloodshed' and the second one was 'The Dust of Hatred in My Eyes' written from the point of view of Bangladesh. Well, that naturally infuriated these people even more. So for a few days, I was obliged to go underground in Sindh and not to stay with the wrath of my patriotic friends. And then the war was over. Pakistan was dismembered.

Because of the elections, the military government was overthrown, and the Bhutto government- People's Party - came into power. I had known him (Bhutto) from the old days, first when he was foreign minister, then when he was leader of the Opposition. He sent for me and said, "What about joining us?" I said, "And do what?" He said, "Look, you have been doing this cultural business, now you do it on the national scale." So I founded the National Council of the Arts, this PNCA, that is here. I formed this and then I formed another institution with the humble name 'Folk Arts,' which is now 'National Institute of Folk Heritage'. I did this for about four years until the government changed. At the same time, I was writing, I wrote three more books; I wrote two or three books of prose and two or three, of poetry. By this time, my works had been translated into English, French, Russian and all sorts of languages. And then, that government was overthrown and the present (Zia-ul-Haq) regime came in. They did not bother me, but so far as the cultural work was concerned, it was not precisely as it was before. Also, I thought I'd better do something else.

Now, during this period, things had happened outside. The organisation for which I had been contributing had taken shape - it was an organisation of African and Asian writers called the Afro-Asian Writers' Association. I had been working for them, attending their meetings and so on. Now they had their headquarters in Cairo, from where they produced a magazine called *Lotus*. After the Camp David Agreement, the Arabs insisted that the office be moved from Cairo, shifted somewhere else. The Chief Editor of this magazine was also the Secretary General. He was shot in Cyprus. So there was nobody else to look after this magazine and no place for a new office. It was decided to set up a new office in Beirut and I was invited to take over this magazine. So I took over this magazine in Beirut, worked for this organisation for four years. And then, of course, we were thrown out.

I managed to slip through the blockade, a month after the city was surrounded and then I came back here. And immediately I fell sick again, after twenty years and well that is the end of the story.

I am sorry I have taken so long, but I could not make it any shorter! Now, the lady asked me whether I would recite some poems. I told her 'I'll tell you a story.' The story is that when I joined the army, for sometime I was posted here in Rawalpindi, which was then the Headquarters of the Northern Command. Here in the garrison at the Northern Headquarters, I was the only Indian officer - the rest were all British. We had a party thrown by one of the British officers. And a dear old lady said, "I hear that you are a poet." I said, "Yes, I plead guilty to that." She said, "How nice! We hope that we'll listen to some poetry after dinner." I said, "I'm sorry, I write in Urdu, my language." She said, "Then why don't you write in English?" I said, "Why should I write in English?" She said, "Isn't it so much easier?"

I am sorry, I do not have my English translations and there are -there is more than one English translation, but I think Pasha has been reading out some things to you. Sorry I took so long, if there is anything else...

Question from audience:

You mentioned falling in love, but you did not mention Alys. (Laughter

from audience).

Faiz: That is right, I forgot! Well, you see, as I told you, that love lasted for seven or eight years. When I started teaching, one of my colleagues, had come from Oxford and was a Marxist and so was his wife. He was also a very good writer. One day she asked me, "Why are you looking so crestfallen? What's wrong? I said, 'Well, look...' She said, "You're in love and suffering from insomnia." I said, "To hell with it!" She said, "You should read this book!" So she gave me two or three books. She said, "What is this small sorrow of yours? Look at the masses of India, they are hungry and they are suffering. What are your sufferings compared to theirs?" Then I stopped with the love thing and began to think of bigger things. That is when I wrote my first poem - 'Don't Ask for More Love'. My colleague, the principal of the college I was working with, had brought with him, from England, an Englishwoman, as his wife and after two or three years, her sister came to see her on a visit to Amritsar, where I was teaching. I met the young lady and we became friends. Then came the War, so she could not go back. In fact, I had also booked my seat to join Cambridge, and so I could not go either. So we became friends and got married, that is where Alys comes in.

Question: Can I ask another personal question? Pasha did give Urdu translations of your poems. Many of them were based in Beirut. In that time, you were talking about, were you living in Beirut, or were you just... (Faiz interrupts)

Faiz: No, no. I was living there all the time.

Question: And were you politically involved in Beirut?

Faiz: I was, indeed, yes! You had to be, if you were part of the suffering of the place and of the people.

Question: Were you attached to a faction?

Faiz: No, no particular faction, but mainly I was working with the Palestinians, who were the people who had been driven out of their homes, people, who were suffering, through no fault of their own.

It was very strange that somebody actually explained it to me as to why and how, the Israelis who had suffered so much under the Nazis, were so brutalized, as far as the Palestinians were concerned. And then, someone explained to me, that if you go through a brutalizing experience, it is a type of suffering that makes you almost lose your compassion and your humanistic instinct. Then, you become equally cruel, like those people who made you suffer, you become a sadist like them, and that is why as far as the Palestinians are concerned, the Israelis have lost all their compassion. Anyway, that was one of the reasons why I got involved with the suffering parties, as normally one does. It is very easy to join the winners, but it is very unproductive, it is much more productive to join the losing side, as far as creativity is concerned.

[Source: "Culture and Identity: Selected English Writings of Faiz," pp. 3-18, Oxford University Press, Karachi, Pakistan]

One-Act Play by Faiz Ahmed Faiz

Private Secretary

Characters:

Hamid
Raheem
Secretary, District Health Board
Shaukat
Jameela
Nawab Ehteshaam-ud-din Khan
Salima
Sarfarosh Jung
Lady Phatak
Voice One
Voice Two
A woman

[Room of a Private Secretary]

Hamid: [Speaking in a tired voice] Twenty four cups of tea. Saucers twenty four, quarter plates twenty four, spoons... [He reaches out to ring the bell. Rahim enters] Rahim, why is it that you are unable to do any work properly? You have not even dusted my table today. All the papers are still scattered all over the room. And for how many days have I been saying that the front window curtain needs to be changed. My eyes hurt at this inconsistency. How can anyone hang a purple curtain on a yellow wall?

Rahim: But Sir, this curtain had been selected by Jamila Madam.

Hamid: [Aside] What possible colour sense can that stupid woman have?

[Coughs loudly] What I mean is that she probably did not pay enough attention to the colour scheme.

Rahim: No Sir, she insists that she is the last word in interior decoration and anyway she is very fond of this colour and this particular shade.

Hamid: Anyway, let that be. Go and find out from the bearer if all the crockery for tea has been laid aside. Tell him to come here and check all these as well.

[Rahim leaves the room and then comes back almost immediately with a card in his hand]

Rahim : Some Sikander Sahab has come to see you. This is his card.

Hamid: [Reading from the card] Secretary, District Health Society. Show him in!

[Rahim leaves the room and the Secretary, District Health Society enters]

Secretary: Adaab Arz!

Hamid: Adaab Arz!

Secretary: I have to meet one Hamid Sahab.

Hamid: I am Hamid. What can I do for you?

Secretary: Can Nawab Sahab, deliver a lecture on the condition of the drains and sewage at the Town Hall, on Sunday?

Hamid : I am afraid, this can be decided by Nawab Sahab himself.

Secretary: But I am coming from his room. He says that he is not very well informed about his schedule and appointments. Please enquire from my Private Secretary. He shall be able to tell you about the subjects on which I shall be able to speak this week.

Hamid: Wonderful! I think that the Nawab has an extremely busy week ahead. There is an extremely important get together this evening, followed by tea. Nawab Sahab's children are to be introduced to important members of high society in this party. I would advise you to postpone this lecture to some later date. This would be convenient for Nawab sahib and also give you more time to make the arrangements.

Secretary: You have a point there. But the trouble is that the Commissioner has agreed to chair the programme. Nawab Sahab seems to think that if this lecture is delivered at the function, it would focus his attention on the subject. The Assembly Elections are drawing near and the selections of the candidates are scheduled to be made soon.

Hamid: If he has already decided and let you know of it then where is the need to ask for my opinion?

Secretary: You are extremely kind. Our society is doing some path breaking work. To date, we have held five such functions. On each occasion more than five resolutions were proposed and twenty of them have been accepted. Four of them have even been published in newspapers.

Hamid: How does it matter what has been published in newspapers? How can that ...

Secretary: Please let me complete what I was saying. After all when Nawab Sahab shall speak from our platform, he should be generous enough to say a few words of praise for us and our work. Otherwise what is our benefit in arranging this function and inviting him to speak? Commissioner Sahib should also learn who we are and what the work is, that we are doing. So as I was saying, our society is doing some extremely beneficial work. Our aim is to make arrangements for the hygiene and cleanliness of the entire town. Every time a senior officer passes through, he does not fail to point out that the markets and shopping areas of this town are disgusting. We want the market places to be gleaming like mirrors. We wish to launch a tirade against filth and disease, people should be made aware about the need for inoculations and ...

Hamid: Look Sir, I am extremely busy at this moment. As I had informed you earlier too, there is an important party this evening and I have the responsibility of making all the arrangements. Since morning I have not had a single moment of peace for myself. In spite of my best efforts, most of the work is still incomplete. Please try and come again some other time, because...

Secretary: But do let me finish what I had started to say. You must have heard our proposals. If it is not too much of a problem, then please note them down. We propose that all the hand carts and cycle rickshaws should be removed from the roads of the town. It is they who reside in the slums, that are the reason for all the dirt in the town. The slums should be bulldozed and beautiful houses should be built on that land. The street vendors and flea market shopkeepers should be taxed and be obliged to get a license for selling their wares and with that...

[Some one knocks on the door]

Hamid: Ugh! What now?

Rahim: [Coming in] Sahabzada Shaukat Sahab is coming!

Hamid: [To the Secretary] I would request you to leave now. Nawab Sahab's son is on his way here and I have to attend to him.

[Sound of footsteps. Shaukat walks in]

Shaukat:[in a grieved tone] But you are the limit, Hamid Sahab. You have not yet written a *ghazal* for me. It is only four hours now from the party and I still have not read it. When do you expect me to learn it?

Hamid: You tell me, where was the time to sit down and write a ghazal? I had to order the crockery, count it, make a list of the eats and order them, write and send out the invitations, visit innumerable restaurants and pastry shops. Believe me, since morning, I have had one foot here and the other at Mall Road.

Shaukat: That is not a good enough excuse. It was not necessary for you to have postponed everything for today. After all, why did you want to write my ghazal on the last day? Nobody seems to have a thought for me.

Hamid: But it has been the same story every day. I reach here early in the mornings every day and then I am on my feet, till eight or nine at night, trying to satisfy everyone here. When I reach home, my body does not even have enough energy, for me to change the clothes. Today I did not even get time to wash my face, leave alone having breakfast. A cup of tea has not touched my lips.

Shaukat: So what am I supposed to do? Tell me, do I have to read out a ghazal in the party or not? Does one need a whole life time to write a few lines? It is such a small, little work, yet you are making a mountain of it!

Hamid: Please do not be upset with me. I have already framed two couplets. In a few minutes I shall write a few more. Five or six couplets would make a complete *ghazal.*

Shaukat: Certainly! And what kind of poetry would this be, that has been written in this off hand manner? Anyway, whichever sort it might be, please have it complete in an hour or so. I have left my friends waiting at the Poker table. See to it that I get the complete piece by the time that I am through with the hand.

Hamid: Rest assured! [Shaukat exits] Allah!...suppose I was to go away somewhere, some place far away. If somehow I am able to shake off this fatigue, in a place of solitude...what was the first line I had thought of? [Begins to hum]

I have given up on the spring yet again
and have wept for so many yet again.

Listen! Get the list of the crockery required. It is still incomplete. Now, till where had I checked and confirmed?...yes, six teapots and six milk pots. [Begins to hum again] But it was not in this desolation that I lost something of life yet again. [Hums again] Big teacups, thirty eight, and small coffee cups, twenty...

Jamila: [Enters the room. She is very agitated] Hamid Sahab, what exactly do you think you are doing? It is now almost noon and the picture in my room, still lies incomplete. You shall not have to face anything, but I will be made a fool of, before all my friends. I am unable to understand why you are so lazy. Now please drop every thing else and go and complete the painting. You treat everything as a joke!

Hamid: This is no laziness, Jamila Bibi. It is not so easy to make a painting. One has to form a picture in one's mind, decide on each line and curve, mix the colours accordingly and then use them on the picture, to have the desired effect.

Jamila: Yes of course, as if I have never seen someone make a painting before. There is an art master at the school, who would willingly paint a picture for anyone for a meagre sum of five rupees. I have seen no one behave as you do.

Hamid: That is a different thing, Jamila Bibi. Even I can copy film posters and make gaudy, loud paintings. But this painting shall carry your name and I do not want your name to be associated with an ordinary art piece that has no aesthetic value. My conscience would not allow me to do such a thing.

Jamila: Now, how does your conscience come in this? You are not going to commit a robbery or any such crime. Why does your conscience have to be concerned with making a painting?

Hamid: You do not understand Jamila Bibi. There is a difference between the everyday morals and creative ethics.

Jamila: Why would I know these intricacies? Quickly finish the painting and see that the standing woman is draped in a red bordered sari. Who wears a blue printed sari? How very unfashionable!

Hamid: This is just not possible. The complete canvas shall be destroyed. It is not possible to adjust the red colour in this painting.

Jamila: What kind of things are you saying today? Are colours like human beings, that they would not be able to adjust to each other? What is so difficult about applying whichever colour one wants, wherever one desires? In any case, the painting is mine and not yours. It shall be made according to my wishes. So please hurry up and do it. It would probably take about ten minutes, on the outside. We are going up to the museum. See that it is complete by the time we return. [Jamila exits]

Rahim: [Enters] Hamid Sahab, Nawab Sahab wants you in his room at once.

Hamid: [Quickly getting up and moving to the door] Allah, help me please!

Rahim: He is here himself.

[Nawab Sahab enters the room]

Hamid: Adaab arz, Sir!

Nawab: Is everything under control? But you are a strange one. Allah knows what the date is today and to date, the appeal of my association has not been sent to the newspapers. The association's annual function is at hand. What date is it?

Hamid: It is the twenty second, Sir...

Nawab: Twenty second. Right. And you have yet to send that telegram to the authorities. The one about the victims of the cyclone. It would be a matter of great shame for me, if someone else was to send a telegram of mourning and request aid for the victims. What is the date today?

Hamid: Twenty second.

Nawab: Yes twenty second. Why didn't you tell me so before? So scribble down the appeal quickly and send it to the papers right away.

Hamid: What should I say Sir?

Nawab: Say that our association has been serving the people for a very long time now. Under this banner, several beneficial projects have been undertaken, and though we have not hand our spreads before anyone...

Hamid: Sir it is ...spread our hands before anyone...

Nawab: Do not interrupt me. Write down whatever I say!

Hamid: Yes, Sir! [Continues writing] Though we have not spread our hand before anyone...

Nawab: That is enough from me. Now give it your mind and complete it yourself. Something to this effect but see to it that the language is ponderous and weighty. And pick up this pile of papers from here. What do you think they are doing here? Cut out the news items that have my name in them and file them. Who knows, we might need some press clippings this evening. Do see that the telegram is sent. So what is the date today?

Hamid: It is twenty second.

Nawab: Then why don't you say so? How many times have I told you to keep the calender right in front of me on my table? I can never remember dates.

Hamid: Sir, it is right before you.

Nawab: True, but you too should keep reminding me. I pay you for that. But wait...I had some other assignment for you...yes of course. There has been a terrible blunder. Shiekh Abid-al-Ghafoor has not been sent the invite for this evening. Why did you not remind me?

Hamid: But Sir, this is the first time I am hearing his name.

Nawab: So this is the level of your information? You do not even know the names of the aristocrats of the city? What are you people being taught in school and college? Shiekh Abid-al-Ghafoor was really upset with me. There is only one way out of this rigmarole. Go personally and deliver the card. You can apologize and say that it was you who forgot to add his name to the list. It is only three miles from here. You shall be back within an hour. Go jump it!

Hamid: But...

Nawab: No buts about it. The young should always be on their toes. Swing over the bicycle and ride on the winds. Jamila is taking the car or else you could have used it. It shall be a bit of trouble but...and yes see that there is no flaw in the arrangements of the party.

Hamid: Yes Sir.

Nawab: Then leave. Why are you looking like a drowned cat? Why are you making me feel as if I have slapped you? Always wear a happy look, understand?

Hamid: Yes, Sir! [Nawab goes out. The sound of a harmonium is heard]

Raheem: Hamid Sahab, Salima Bibi is waiting for you. [Opens the door for Salima]

Salima: Where had you vanished? I have been waiting for so long. I have prepared that song. All you have to do is hear it once.

Hamid: [Fed up and irritated] Maybe later, Salima Bibi! I have no time now.

Salima: Wonderful! When shall you have the time? It is already one in the afternoon. Merely three hours left.

Hamid: Then you could sing one of the earlier songs. You can see that all the arrangements are still half done. I still have to go down to Nanak Chand for the sweets. It would take me almost two hours. Suppose there was a flaw in the arrangements of the party, then I would be done for.

Salima: I know nothing about that. I have worked so hard for two hours to memorise this wretched song and you say that I should sing an old one? I refuse to accept this. Sit down and listen to me now! [She begins to sing and is very off note] *This is a world full of lies...*

Hamid: No, not like this. You must listen properly...[Sings]...*This is a world full of lies, my friend...*

Shaukat: [Enters and speaks in his earlier manner] Hamid Sahab, is my ghazal complete?

Hamid: Ugh! Do forgive me! Just give me five minutes and I shall complete it.

Shaukat: Look I cannot waste five minutes, waiting for you. My friends are waiting for me.

Hamid: Then please come back after some time.

Shaukat: You think I have no other work but to keep making rounds of this room? You have spoilt our entire game of cards.

Hamid: Then do wait for a few minutes and I shall write it down for you.

Salima: But do attend to my song before doing anything else.

Hamid: Yes, yes, please sing on. [Salima again sings in that off note and repeats the first line again and again. Sometimes Hamid's humming can also be heard.]

Hamid: [Softly] What was the wretched rhyme? [To Salima] Excellent. Please continue ... it is perfect.

Salima: Thank you!

Hamid: [Continues to hum the ghazal] *And I found myself sitting near you yet again.* Here Shaukat Sahab...your *ghazal* is done.

Shaukat: Right! Now let me memorise it. But...this is only five couplets. Why is it so short? And it does not seem to be very lyrical either. Anyway, it shall have to do, since you can't come up with a better one. Now tell me the tune in which I shall render it.

Hamid: For the love of Allah! Have some mercy on me, Shaukat Sahib. I still have to do thousands of things.

Shaukat: So you think this is no work? Then I shall have to complain to Daddy.

Hamid: Ugh! Alright, sing with me. [He begins to sing and Shaukat joins him in a loud, cracked voice]

Hamid: Exactly! That is how it has to be sung. Please let me go now so that I can reach Nanak Chand in time.

Shaukat: But hear the complete *ghazal.*

Hamid: There is no need. You are perfect. Rahim, tell the waiters to arrange all the things on the table, themselves. You keep an eye on it. I am going till Nanak Chand's shop. It is more than three miles from here. I might be a bit late for the party.

Rahim: How will you go in this heat, Sir? Outside, the sun is beating down, with all its might. Even the thought of venturing out at this hour is frightening.

Hamid: What can't be helped has to be borne. The heat and the cold are only for the rich. How can it affect people like you and me? All weather is working weather for us!

Rahim: At least take an umbrella. There is one in my room. You shall get a heatstroke.

Hamid: How shall I carry an umbrella on bicycle, my stupid friend? If anyone asks for me, tell them that I have gone out.

Rahim: Right, Sir.

[A short gap in which, the tinkle of crockery can be heard. The clock strikes four. Sound of cars, driving up and stopping. Sounds of laughter and discussion. The voices merge with each other. The ring of the telephone is heard again and again. Alternatively these names are also heard... Kalandar Ali Khan, Sarfaroz Jung, Nawab Tajjamil Hussain Khan, Raibahadur Ganga Prashad, Kunwar Inderjeet Singh, Khan Bahadur Mushtaq Ahmed Khan, Miss Jane Bernard, Miss Shiela Rattan, Sir Phaatak Chand.

Sarafaroz : Adaab Arz! So how do you do, Nawab Sahab?

Shaukat Sahab ushers in Miss Bernard and takes her to a sofa. The telephone rings. "Do attend to the phone Shaukat Mian". Noise of spoons and other cutlery and crockery

Lady Phatak : I suppose everyone has arrived now. Do call your children Nawab Sahab.

All: Yes, yes, do call your children.

Nawab: Ladies and gentleman, it is a source of great pleasure for me that all of you have honoured me with your presence. My children are but like your own children. They shall prosper in this world with your help and support. I do not wish to take a lot of time. I request Sarfaroz Jung to be kind enough to chair this outing...I mean this function...no this programme and shall call his children...no my children.

Sarfaroz: We shall first have a song from Miss Salima. [Claps. Salima sings the song.]

A Voice: Wonderful! Marvelous!

Hamid: Disgusting!

A Woman : Did you say something Hamid Sahab?

Hamid: No, Not really!

A Woman: Are you fond of music?

Hamid: No, Madam.

Sarfaroz: Now Jamila Bibi shall show you a painting that she has recently completed.

Jamila: [Giggling and trying to show off] Look at this painting. It is not my best one though. I think this sari should have been red, but...well...it has come out this way...

A Voice: But this is remarkable. The painting seems to come alive. We must congratulate you, dear Jamila. You must be so proud, Nawab Sahab.

Sarfaroz: Now Sahabzada Shaukat Sahab shall recite his latest *ghazal* to you.

Shaukat: I wish you all Adaab Arz. [Begins to sing in the off note, cracked voice]

A Voice: But really, he is a very good poet.

Another Voice: Remarkable. Each couplet is balanced and beautiful.

Third Voice: Just see the rhymes and the use of symbols.

First Voice: Nawab Sahab, you are really blessed. One of your daughters, is such a good singer, the second is a painter and your son is a capable poet. You, by Allah's grace, are a known scholar and respected intellectual. You have really nurtured the talents of your children.

Sarfaroz: But friends, this programme seems to have ended very soon. Why doesn't someone else recite some poetry?

A Female Voice: Hamid Sahab, you also look as if you are fond of poetry. Why don't you read out some of your poems?

Hamid: No Madam! I would rather not.

Second voice: Stop being so shy. We are all friends here.

Sarafaroz: Now that I think of it, I have seen you in gatherings of poets at *mushairas.* Why don't you read out something to us?

Hamid: I would beg to be excused for now.

Many voices: No, no, we insist, please read out something. Please keep quiet. Give him some peace to collect his thoughts. [Sound of clapping]

Hamid: [In a soft, lost voice, that hides a deep anger in it] You wish to hear my poems?

[Shouts of 'certainly, certainly' are heard]

Hamid: From me? [Voices shout in the affirmative]

Hamid: [Suddenly, with passion] Shall I recite some of my poems? And just now, whose poetry was it, that was being murdered? Do you believe for a minute that this son of a gorilla can write such delicate thoughts? A fool, who has no other work but to play cards and sit and gossip over endless rounds of tea, can create the couplets that he just read out?

Shaukat: Don't talk nonsense!

Voices: What? Really? Is it possible? But this is criminal!

Another voice: Impossible! How can anyone do this to an artist?

Nawab: [Trying to redeem the situation] I think this young man is a bit fatigued. You see, he has made all the arrangements for this party. They were extremely well made, my dear fellow but I think they have taken their toll of you. Please take some rest.

Hamid: Some rest? You think, some rest can reclaim my self esteem? Do you think a couple of days off, shall bring me round to again become your shoe licking, private secretary?

Sarfaroz: Young man, do take a hold of yourself and tell us what has happened.

Hamid: [Trying to control himself] There is nothing to narrate. I am a Private Secretary and hence am always being shoved around. I myself do not know whose Private Secretary I am.

Jamila: He is just an incompetent fool who does not even know how to paint a blue sari red in a painting.

Nawab: Shut up!

Salima: Yes, he did not even want to teach me this song.

Nawab: Keep quiet. Will you?

Many Voices: So this painting has been made by this young man? Oh the shame of it!

Another Voice: And this girl has learnt this song from you?

Sarfaroz: Good God! Is that true, Hamid?

Hamid: Why are you so shocked? It is something that takes place all the time in this world. People with no money have to sell what they can. In my case, it is my poetry and artistic skill. But I refuse to be abused anymore. I am done with vending my talents, to fill my stomach.

A Voice: What then do you propose to do? Are you giving up this job?

Hamid: Yes. Now, immediately!

A Voice: If you like you can work for me. I would like to have a private secretary of your calibre.

Hamid: Thank you, but no. I am done with selling my talents, whatever be the price paid for them. I shall rather be unemployed and sell vegetables on a hand cart than auction my poems and paintings. Let hunger be my companion than bread bought at the cost of my creativity. I know that it is going to be a hard life, full of all kinds of struggle, but it shall bring me the fulfillment of having nurtured my artistic expertise. I shall have the satisfaction of not having sold it to the highest bidder.

[Translation from Urdu to English : Noor Zaheer]

Ludmila Vasilieva*

Spoilt child of fortune who worked very hard

The story of our fathers, Like a story from the age of the Stuarts, More distant than Pushkin; And it is seen as if in a dream - ***Boris Pasternak***

From among the compatriots of Faiz Ahmed Faiz, who chose writing as their profession, it would be hard to find anyone so favoured by providence. 'Spoilt child of fortune' was the name that some of his critics gave him. To some extent they were right, but it should be borne in mind that Faiz was above all, someone who worked hard.

One of the tragedies, which, in all ages has beset the 'Prophet-Poet' - that traditionally dramatic figure of society - is that, people of his own time have neither heard nor listened to his voice, and his verse has found due recognition only from those who have come after him. But in this regard, Faiz was much more fortunate than many of his predecessors and even many of his talented contemporaries. He was not only heard and listened to, but was also loved and adored, and during his own lifetime, he was elevated to the ranks of the classic writers of Urdu poetry.

The sky above him, however, was not always without its clouds. Thunder and lightning often resounded over his head; storms of malevolence and violence crashed into his life, which on more than one occasions, was threatened by mortal danger. But this only served to temper the poet's spirit and burnished the gold of his glory. Fortune itself, was gracious to Faiz, as indeed it was at one time, to his father.

---

* Ludmila Vasilieva is a Professor of Urdu literature at Institute of Oriental Studies, Moscow, Russia.

Faiz's father, Sultan Muhammad Khan, a lawyer from the small Punjab town of Sialkot, was an extraordinary individual. The events of his life remind us more of some fantastic fairy-tale than of the humdrum existence of a provincial advocate. The upheavals of his fortunes inspired the English author Lillias Hamilton to write the novel 'A Vizier's Daughter', which was based on the actual events of Sultan Muhammad's life. The novel was published from London, in 1900.

One of the most notable traits in his character, an ambition always to have the very best, combined with a fighting instinct, helped Sultan Muhammad to achieve his place in the sun. It was not for nothing that, in the family, the legend was current, that his ancestors had been Kshatriya warriors, belonging to the Hindu martial caste, who could trace their origins back to Rajput princes with the clan name of Sen Pal. It is difficult to say when exactly and in what circumstances the family embraced Islam, but it is known for certain that Sultan Muhammad's grandfather bore the name of Sarbuland, indicating that he belonged to the Muslim faith, and that his father was called Sahibzada Khan. Sultan was born to a family of poor peasants in the village of Kalakadir, not far from Sialkot. From there he began his journey *per ardua ad astra* - through hardships, to the stars.

The house in which Faiz's father was born, was so poor that in order to economize, the kerosene lamp burnt in the evenings only, for the shortest possible time. The idea of having the children educated was entirely out of the question, but Sultan was born with the proverbial silver spoon in his mouth. From his early childhood, the boy was obliged to earn his own living and even to bring the family a small hunk of bread, he tended the village herd. While looking after the cattle of his fellow-villagers, Sultan saw with envy and dismay, the boys, who were the same age as he, hurrying off to school, but one day, able to bear it no longer, he left the herd to the care of Allah and stole away behind the other children, to the class.

The teacher, like a kindly magician, not only took pity on the poor cowherd, who dreamt of an education, but even played a part in his fate. From that day onwards, Sultan began to hurry off to the school every morning, clutching his homework, which he would hand to the teacher for correction, and upon receiving a fresh assignment, would return to his duties as a herdsman. The teacher, overjoyed at the boy's success, obtained permission for him to sit in the examinations for a course in the elementary school. Sultan's results turned out to be the best, from among all the other pupils. As a reward, he was given a monthly allowance of some two rupees. For a poor family, this was a considerable amount of money, and now Sultan was able to enter the middle school, which was situated in another village, several kilometres from Kalakadir. For a number of years, the boy had to go back and forth on foot, in all weathers, but in his unquenchable thirst for knowledge, he paid hardly any attention to such inconveniences.

Sultan finished middle school with the same distinction, and for this reason he managed to go on to pursue his studies, in the city of Lahore. In those days, pilgrims and poor students could find temporary accommodation in the mosques, and lived on the charity donated by the local people. Sultan had another stroke of good fortune and set himself up in one of these hostels. Rather than live on charity, after finishing his lessons, the young student went to the mosque and took any work that was going. He had an attractive appearance, was polite, courteous and naturally tactful, and all this invariably inspired in his associates, a liking for the young man. Apart from anything else, he possessed an uncommonly pleasant voice, and soon he was appointed to read the Koran at the time of prayer. But in the evenings, he often walked to the station and worked as a porter so that he might send at least a little money home to his parents, in the village. Such an intense daily routine, however, did not prevent Sultan from doing as brilliantly as ever, in his studies. He was particularly gifted in languages, and quickly mastered the subtleties of English and Persian and was able to speak both of them, fluently.

One day, fortune smiled upon him again. The Afghan ambassador, Amir Muhammad Khan, came to the mosque to take part in the Friday prayers. Along with the other attendants in the mosque, Sultan, who had long been regarded as part of the community, was introduced to the honoured guest. The tall, well-proportioned young man, with handsome features, greeted the ambassador in his own language and did not remain unnoticed. During the conversation, it became clear that the young man had also mastered English, the language which the Afghan ambassador intended to study. Apparently Sultan had made a great impression on the guest. A high-ranking official of the Emir soon invited him to become a tutor in his house.

From this point, events proceeded like those of a real fairy-tale. When the noble grandee returned to his homeland, he took Sultan, to whom he had become very attached, along with him. In Kabul, Sultan's patron introduced him to the King of Afghanistan himself, Amir Abdurrahman. The quick-witted and handsome young boy, at once gained the king's favour and procured for himself the post of court translator. His duties were to translate documents, received from British into Persian and to render the Emir's replies to them into English. Amir Abdurrahman, seeing his intelligence and zeal, showered him with royal favours. Indeed, Sultan Muhammad lost count of the valuable presents he received in precious jewels and money. One day he was appointed as chief secretary to the court, or in other words he became the 'royal vizier'. By degrees he rose higher and higher, and eventually became tutor to the son of the heir to the throne.

Fairy-tales relate not only their hero's flight beyond the clouds and his ascent to the summits of riches, fame and glory; but sooner or later evil forces conspire in the events. It is hardly surprising that among the king's courtiers, there were many, who envied and resented the young man, and who could not bear to witness the magical career of this foreign upstart. In the court, plots started to be hatched against him, but even at this point, Fortune did not desert her favoured child.

At the royal court, Sultan Muhammad met Lillias Hamilton, a most distinguished and influential person. Some considered her to be a relation or even a niece of Queen Victoria. The bright personality of the young foreigner made a strong impression upon her. She kept a close eye on the intrigues that were being woven around him, and about which he apparently had not the slightest suspicion. Lillias Hamilton managed to warn Sultan about these plots, and advised him to leave Afghanistan before the monarch's favour could turn to enmity. Sultan followed her advice without hesitation. Lillias even took upon herself, the task of looking after his affairs, and all his money was immediately transferred to her account, in a London bank.

After leaving Afghanistan in secret, Sultan made his way to Lahore, but there he attracted the suspicions of the British authorities, was arrested and thrown into prison, in the Lahore Fort. By a quirk of fate, many years later, his son, Faiz Ahmed, would become an inmate of that very same fort. An inquiry was started. Sultan Muhammad managed to inform Lillias Hamilton, who was now in London, about his misfortune. Once more, she came to the aid of this erstwhile vizier, entered into correspondence with the British authorities in Lahore, and shortly Sultan Muhammad was released.

On the advice of his benefactress, Sultan Muhammad Khan left Lahore for London, where the next fantastic episode of his life began. He received the considerable sum of money, which had been transferred from Afghanistan, and began to live the life of a habitue of fashionable salons. He had his own equipage, and frequented clubs, gaming houses and other extravagant places of amusement. In spite of all this, however, he never lost his passion for learning. He entered Cambridge University, and after successfully finishing his course there, he took a diploma in law, which enabled him to open his own chambers. It is worth noting that at the same time many future leading figures in the history of India were receiving their legal training in Cambridge, and among them was Muhammad Iqbal. Sultan was on friendly terms with all of them.

When the Emir of Afghanistan discovered that his favourite fugitive had turned up in London, he offered him the post of Afghanistan's ambassador to Britain. Sultan Muhammad Khan readily accepted, and ambassadorial status opened the door to the most influential houses in the country. He gained an audience with Queen Victoria and was accepted as a member of the Royal Geographical Society. One of his polo partners was the Duke of Windsor. Sultan Muhammad arranged magnificent receptions, glittering balls and sumptuous banquets. Such exotic features of his house as his harem added further to the curiosity of the members of the London aristocracy and attracted their attention towards him. In short, Sultan Muhammad shone in English high society and at that time, it seemed that his whole life had become one perpetual starlit hour.

But alas! The end of Sultan's stay in England resembled the conclusion of the parable of the prodigal son. The high life-style he adopted, soon ruined our oriental dandy, and it was not long before his famous friends and acquaintances lost interest in him, no longer seeking his company. Not surprisingly, he soon fell out with them, and finally had no other choice than to return to his native land.

At first, Sultan Muhammad settled in the little town of Jhelum, where he tried to establish a legal practice, but Jhelum was far too small, and in the absence of sufficient work, he was obliged to move to Sialkot. In the land of his birth, the father of the future poet was plunged into a round of the most amazing adventures and wanderings.

In Sialkot, it seems that his affairs once more improved. In all events, after a few years, the former vizier, recalling his earlier escapades, again began to live in style.

Sultan Muhammad Khan was married more than once. Zafar ul Hasan, the author of a number of works on Faiz, insists that he married twice, the second time after the death of his first wife. This, however, is not in accordance with other reliable accounts. Some sources claim that he contracted three marriages, and a few state that he married five times. The exact number of Sultan's marriages does not concern us here, but what can be said for sure is that his first wife was the niece of the Afghan Emir. She died two years after the marriage took place. Again, it is certain that his last wife, the youngest of all, whom he married when he had already settled down in Sialkot, was the mother of Faiz. Her name was Sultan Fatima, the daughter of a powerful landowner. According to Faiz, during his childhood there was at least one other wife in the family, who, in keeping with the custom observed in polygamous Muslim households, was known as 'elder mother'. Alys Faiz, the widow of the poet, in her autobiography 'Over my Shoulder', mentions that Faiz's father had been married several times before being wed to Sultan Fatima: 'His wives had been impoverished Kabul princesses, and the last wife who came to his home was the same age as his eldest daughter.' In their letters, Alys and Faiz mention 'Mother of Bali' (a short form of Iqbal), Faiz's stepsister, with whom Alys was on very friendly terms, though Faiz never referred to her as 'elder mother'. It is possible that the reference was to one of the wives of Faiz's father.

In Sultan Muhammad Khan's huge house, there was always a large number of people, and life centred around the *zananakhana*, the women's quarters into which, male strangers were not even allowed to peep. When the younger children made a noise, their elders, in an attempt to calm them, told them that it was bad to make such a row. In the house they really preferred silence and calm. In her memoirs, Alys Faiz writes about the 'royal persons of Kabul', meaning Sultan Muhammad's Kabul female relations, whom she refers to as 'women of the house, whispering in Persian'. Besides women and children, there were aunts, nephews and nieces, male and female cousins. The head of the family fed them all, took care of them and looked after them.

The family grew up and children were born. In 1911, a boy came into the world to whom, they gave the name of Faiz.

In this large family, nothing was ever in short supply. The daughters lived in the lap of comfort and plenty, and the growing sons were educated in the most prestigious establishments. The house was always full of relations and friends. Fortune had smiled once more on her favourite son.

In 1931, a clap of thunder resounded in the clear sky; Sultan Muhammad Khan died suddenly. Only then did it become clear that for many years the family had been living on credit. The sole legacy of the late master of the house was a string of huge debts. At once, a host of creditors and moneylenders came running up. The bereaved family had nothing with which to settle its debts. All the financial affairs had been conducted by the head of the household, and it was always considered unseemly to talk about money at home. The death of Sultan Muhammad brought financial ruin to this outwardly prosperous family; in a matter of days, the cousins, nieces and nephews found other places of refuge, and only the most helpless and vulnerable members remained in the house. At the time of his father's death, Faiz, who had just turned twenty, was studying in Lahore, and had three more years to go, before completing his higher education. Concerned for the good name of his late father, the eldest brother, Tufail, sold off almost the whole of the estate, in order to pay off his father's debts. The members of his family were left penniless and practically without a roof over their heads, and they had no other means of support. For a paltry sum, Tufail rented a small dwelling, in which from that day onwards, the family lived, cooped up together.

During his lifetime, Sultan Muhammad had put a substantial sum of money into the purchase of land around his native village, which he had assigned to the use of local peasants, who were in some way, his kinsmen. After his death, the whole of this landed property was found to be in the hands of these distant relations. Tufail turned to them and made it clear to them that the family's financial position could only be saved by selling off this land. But the village relations had not the slightest intention of returning it to its rightful owner. In fairness, it was hardly proper to suspect them of trying to make profit or of desiring to take advantage of the misfortunes of their relations, from the town. These peasants had probably become used to regarding these plots of land as their own property. After alI, they have been brought up by Sultan, their successful and fabulously wealthy kinsman. Apart from that, they had nowhere else to go. Indeed, this land, which had been watered by the sweat of several generations of farmers, was their home!

When the question of court proceedings was raised, Faiz, one of the legal heirs, at once refused to take part in the litigation. But Tufail, who had the whole burden of these extremely difficult family problems on his shoulders, as well as the task of partially financing the education of his younger brother, was otherwise inclined. He submitted a petition to the court demanding that the land be returned to the direct heirs of the late owner. His resolve was made all the more firm by the feelings of guilt that he had towards his mother, who had been obliged to sell off her jewellery in order to acquire the sum necessary for furthering Faiz's studies. In Indian families, women's jewels, which are usually passed on to their daughters, were regarded as a symbol of the family's prosperity. Selling them, was the last resort in coping with critical situations. The reason for Tufail's anguish was that, as the eldest son, he was unable to save his mother from taking this desperate course of action.

It would be unfair not to point out that Sultan Muhammad Khan's contact with the villagers had always been close, and gifts from the land were sent to the Sialkot home not only during the lifetime of the master, but even after his death. When the struggle for the ownership of the land was proceeding, the 'defendants' could not bear to see their relations from the town, who were almost reduced to beggary, going hungry. From the village they continued to send grain, vegetables, peas, ghee (clarified butter) and other kinds of food.

The legal wrangling over the land went on for years. Tufail eventually won the case, but was unable to release the land from the families settled upon it. He died in 1952 from a heart attack in Hyderabad (Sindh) before he could meet Faiz, who at that time, was in prison, on a charge of conspiracy against the state. The saga of the land was brought to a conclusion by a forthright decision taken by Faiz, after his release from jail, in 1955. To everyone's satisfaction, he claimed for himself only his father's house in the village and a small part of the land surrounding it, but made the rest of the land over to those relations, who had been working and living upon it.

At last, even Faiz's mother, who was a native of those parts, could be completely reconciled with her kinsfolk, with whom relations had been strained during the land dispute. Sultan Fatima, once more, had the chance to travel, at any time, to the village she loved with all her heart and to live in the house where she had spent the first years of her married life, and where her second son, Faiz Ahmed Faiz, had been born. Recalling those days, Faiz writes: 'Mother tenderly embraced me again and again; she kissed me and repeated: "Faiz, my little son! How clever you were, to find such a way out!"

Sultan Muhammad had nine children from different wives - four sons and five daughters. In his large family, no difference was ever made between his own and his stepchildren. Faiz had the closest relationship with his brother Tufail and his sister Bibigul. Thanks to Biblgul, a number of hitherto unknown biographical facts about her brother were rediscovered. In the literature on Faiz, frequent reference is made to the information supplied by her .

Faiz survived two of his brothers and three of his sisters, but the greatest blow he suffered, the pain of which lasted the whole of his life, was the death of his brother Tufail, who was only three years older than Faiz.

This description of the father and the ancestral home of the poet would not be complete without some account of Sialkot, Faiz's home town, which is situated in the north east of Punjab. The town, now counted among the ten largest in Pakistan, in terms of its antiquity can vie with many cities of the Indo-Pakistan subcontinent, and much research has been devoted to it. The author of one of these studies, the historian, writer and journalist Muhammad Din Fauq, a contemporary and friend of Iqbal, writes that the town was founded, some five thousand years ago, by Raja Shal and is mentioned in the Mahabharata, as a place on the banks of the Upkonda, situated in the country of Madra. It is exactly in this region, according to one of the legends of the Mahabharata, that a beautiful daughter, Savitri, was born to the ruler of Madra, Raja Ashvapati Savitri, the eternal epitome of conjugal devotion and overcame the god of Death himself, the terrible Yama, in single combat, for the life of her husband, the noble Satyavan. Most likely, there, in the mists of time, lies hidden the inexhaustible source of the fidelity, the self-sacrifice and the spiritual beauty of the daughters of this land, the protectors of the ancestral hearth, women like the mother of Faiz.

During the age of Chandragupta Vikramaditya, the ruler of the town, SMI Babhan, built a fortress there, which was eventually called Shal-kot. In the course of time, the name was changed into Sialkot, which the town bears to this day.

The history of the town is not only connected to Hindu, but also to many Muslim tales and legends. The heroes of some of these are the old saints, the wise and pious sheikhs, the *sufi* dervishes, who knew the secrets of existence, and the martyrs of Islam, who now rest beneath the domes of the tombs and gravestones, scattered around the old fort of Sialkot.

In Sialkot's chronicles, there are pages which describe the uprising of the military garrison of the town in July 1857, which formed part of the first organised protest against British colonial rule, better known in English as the Sepoy Mutiny of 1857-9. After the fall of Delhi, even the resistance of the Punjab provinces was broken, including that of Sialkot. An enormous fine of 50,000 rupees was imposed upon the inhabitants of the town, two garrison officers were hanged, and 139 soldiers were tied to the muzzle of a cannon and shot - the typical means of British execution in India.

Such was the glorious past of the town as recorded in historical chronicles and legends. Towards the beginning of the twentieth century, Sultan Muhammad settled in Sialkot and contracted his last marriage, and it was here that three of his sons were born. The middle son, Faiz Ahmed Faiz, was destined to become a poet, second in fame only to the Poet of the East, Muhammad Iqbal.

Ashok Vajpeyi*

Wounds of Reality on a Romantic Self-Some Notes on Faiz

As we celebrate the birth centenary of Faiz it is evident that here is a poet whose impact and presence pervade far outside his language. There are many lessons one could learn from the irrepressible romanticism and an equally powerful political consciousness of Faiz.

Faiz belongs to a global category of people who had to suffer suppression and exile and which includes Nazim Hikmat, Czelaw Milosz, Joseph Brodsky, Pablo Neruda, Mahmud Dervish, etc. A question has been raised quite often whether political activism, commitment, devotion to any ideology etc. harm poetry or inevitably make it narrow, predictable and parochial. One answer is that lesser poets are hurt by such ideological commitment, since they expect and demand concessions on the basis of their ideological loyalty and many a time, succeed to gain recognition on that basis. But, in the case of a major poet, ideological orientation does sustain and vitalise his/her human intensity and involvement: ideology does not restrict him, it liberates him. Whenever necessary, a major poet could break open any case of ideas or ideologies. He becomes a major poet since he, if necessary, dares to question his own vision and ideological commitment. The vision of a major poet cannot be fully and honestly contained in any ideology. If his poetry were unable to develop and assert its own vision, it would stop short of being major in any case. Like Faiz, Muktibodh and Shamsher, two Hindi masters have been glowing instances of such daring. Contradictions are untenable and unacceptable in ideology: they are almost natural and inevitable in major poetry. In our times a poetry bent upon consistency to any ideology, can hardly hope to be major

---

* Ashok Vajpeyi is the Chairman of Lalit Kala Academy, New Delhi, a distinguished poet, critic and writer.

since it would, then, lack alertness to the times we are living and caught in. In this context, it is well worth remembering that while each ideology has its limitations and exclusions, not all ideologies are uniformly so. Some do allow plurality and in literature, they alone nurture creativity. Also, a withdrawal from ideology does not amount to withdrawal from ideas. If there is major poetry, Stephen Spender clarified years ago, the ideas behind it can only be major ideas. Major ideas may not always inspire major poetry but there can be no major poetry, which has minor or trivial ideas behind it.

In many languages and literatures of India, it is believed, under a somewhat mistaken impact of the West, that tradition and change are mutually antagonistic. Faiz assumes significance since he stuck to tradition but bent it to the needs of time, making it vulnerable and open to change. This re-invention, as it were, of tradition makes him a poet both of his times and beyond. One of the reasons, for his long-standing and widespread popularity in the subcontinent is that he practiced the conventional mode of poetic utterance in Urdu with dexterity and brought about many changes and variations, in subtle ways, thereby ensuring easy communication.

The wide impact of and admiration for Faiz's poetry is also evidence of the fact that the partition of the subcontinent, a political and, in many ways, disastrous act, failed to divide it culturally: the languages could not be and were, in fact, not partitioned; only territory and geography were divided but not culture. Through Faiz's poetry, we, in India, are able to transgress both political and territorial borders. No other poet either from India or Pakistan, enjoys such distinction, as Faiz does. In one of his early couplets Faiz had said:

> One moves from the entire world
>
> when one sits close beside you
>
> ....
>
> O Faiz, let things take their own course
>
> you'd better keep spinning out verses

In spite of this early intention, Faiz did not spend his later life watching whatever was happening and ensconcing it in verse. His poetry, on the contrary, watches and registers his times and society and constantly seeks and longs for alternative times and society. This is a poetry in which what is and what happens, are forever poised vis a vis what is not and what could happen. That which is, is, simultaneously, under the shadow, in a manner of speaking, of that which is not.

In the Indian sub-continental, tradition poetry has been celebrative, though, doubts have also invariably been creeping in. On the one hand, you have some excesses of emotion, on the other, there is intellectual toughness. For poetry, reality is always soiled which it refuses to divide or see in white and black. This greyness makes the texture of poetry itself, somewhat stained. Aspiring for light, we cannot bypass or disregard the growing and surrounding darkness. Faiz recognized this very early. He had dared to write at the time of independence in 1947:

> This daybreak, pockmarked ...
> this morning night bitten.
> Surely, this is not the morning we'd longed for

One of the major and abiding respects of the 20th century has been that it has made, keeping vigil on freedom, equality and justice an essential function of poetry. In these unfortunate times, poetry resists the shrinking of conscience, warns us about the threats to it and to the extent possible, has been endeavoring to save it. The poetry of Faiz, in its best moments, raises the voice of conscience. This real politics resides in this voice for which any frame of or allegiance to any ideology is strictly not necessary. Poetry must aspire to change but poetry cannot change anything-poetry makes nothing happen-have been polarities for long creating much complexity and some confusion. They have become sharper in our times. But it cannot be gainsaid that Faiz did contribute towards creating a political ethos, desiring change. Poetry cannot bring about change but, perhaps, it can intensify the desire for change and also reveal its possibility. It can rekindle the hope that a world better than the given one is possible and that it is within our powers to bring it about. This belief is very evident in the lines of his poem "Tarana-2":

We will witness

We will witness the day ordained

Not only this but after asserting that 'the crowns will be tossed, thrones will be brought down', the poem ends with these lines:

Only The name will survive

Who cannot be seen but is also present

Who is the spectacle and the beholder, both

I am the Truth- the cry will rise,

Which is I, as well as you

And then God's creation will rule

Which is I, as well as you

It is not coincidental that these lines were used by Pakistani singers to express their resistance to the military rule and to rouse the people against it. It cannot be overstated that the poetry of Faiz had emerged, in the non-democratic politics of Pakistan, as a powerful political opposition. Even in India, in spite of its thriving democracy, poetry has been, in the last 50 years or so, a kind of opposition, though it never got that kind of social and cultural sanction that Faiz's poetry attained, in Pakistani society and system.

Saying 'It was we who were killed in the dark alleys', Faiz still manages to put together an architecture of hope. In agonizing times, when all dreams and utopias seemed to have been thrown into the dustbin of history, Faiz did not look for them in some other world. A major poet does not transport us to another world. He makes us see and seek light in the self-same darkening and stained world of ours. There are times when, in a society, poetry or literature attains the status of conscience. In many totalitarian regimes, including both the Nazi and the Soviet systems, this did happen. For instance, in Poland, which was suppressed for decades by tyrannical regimes, Czeslaw Milosz and Zbigniew Herbert were widely seen and functioned as the conscience, the 'aesthetic conscience' of the Polish people. Faiz also, similarly, emerged as conscience for the people of Pakistan.

One of the jobs of poetry is to keep vigil on words and language, on humanity and its incredible plurality. It keeps them in animation and stiffly opposes and resists any meddling with or reduction in them. Faiz did carry out this function admirably. He kept alive, the Urdu tradition, in its passionate intensity, and reformed it to face new challenges and to cope with them. This could be termed as radicalisation of a tradition, its imaginative and courageous expansion. He could articulate with ease something profound:

> What good is a verse
> that does not light up the world?
> What good a tearful eye
> if it does not wash away the city?

This radicalisation adds to the cultural freedom of the society. Many a times he seemed to have compensated the inadequacy of actual freedom with this expansion and made it real for the lovers of his poetry. Many of them were under several political restrictions but his poetry gave them a kind of spiritual freedom. There are dark times when poetry remains the only site of freedom. In India, during our freedom struggle poetry did emerge as such a site. After independence Faiz's poetry, in his social milieu, did become such a site.

Faiz's romanticism is a crucial aspect of his poetry. It would not be wrong to say that his politics has emerged out of this romantic vision rather than the other way round. He has no hesitation in saying:

> I have made my life simple
> I have only loved
> or,
> When ugliness of the world becomes oppressive
> I wish to write odes to beautiful women

Generally, nostalgia is not thought of as desirable in our century, since somehow it makes us gloat on the past. But in Faiz, not only is there unrestrained fulsome romanticism; his poetry makes nostalgia, a loving and palatable state of mind:

> What beautiful spectacles used to pass before our eyes
> it was only a matter of few days ago
> How bright our lanes used to become
> when my love walked through it

The romantic verve of Faiz is not merely a version of dreaminess. In its texture, a lot of reality is also skillfully woven. The romantic self feels the wounds of reality on its body and makes them manifest. Going from the 'alley of the beloved' to the 'gallows' is not merely a sad recognition of hard cruel reality. While in the jail, Faiz could assert: 'The evening of sorrow is of course prolonged, but it is mere evening'. In spite of all the constraints, his hope never dies:

> The songs of sorrow that I sing in cage
> have become expression of every one in the garden

Frequently he consoles himself, with this hope:

> The morning breeze knocks at the prison door once again
> And says dawn approaches do not loose heart

By saying 'The pain of struggle for life is more baffling than the pain of separation' he does accept the temptations of the other reality. But it would not be fair to say that either as a poet or a person, he ever allowed reality to supersede his dreams. In him, the dreams continued to be pierced with reality but they were never defeated by it. Now, when there is a general acceptance and acknowledgment of many different kinds of modernity, specific to their times and locations, Faiz could be remembered as one of the architects of the sub-continental modernity, which endeavoured to reinvent tradition and which refused to marginalise the romantic spirit and emotional verve under the 'terrorism of the intellect'. For Faiz, the romantic is almost the only part of the classical, worth inheriting: for him the romantic is essentially classical. He should not be connected to Pablo Neruda and Nazim Hikmet, merely because they all shared Marxist ideology. More importantly, all the three distanced themselves from the Western high modernism, which negated the romantic sensibility and, instead, made the romantic carry the modern. This romantic sensibility had the capacity, both to dream and to stare at reality: it was inclusive and had the creative capacity, to carry local traditions as well. It is not without reason, that Faiz could only be in this subcontinent, just as Nazim could only be in Turkey and Neruda in Latin America.

I had the opportunity of meeting Faiz twice and knowing a bit of him. I first met him when he visited Bhopal. His host was my poet-friend Fazal Taabish, who was the then Secretary of Urdu Akademi of Madhya Pradesh and it was he who invited him to Bhopal. By that time he had been widely recognized as a major poet in Urdu. Thousands gathered to listen to his poetry. In spite of his vast popularity, Faiz used to be a little indifferent towards his poetry. He read with some indifference, his own verses as if he was reading somebody else's poetry. I teased him later that he had taken the famous 'alienation principle' of Bertolt Brecht, originally prescribed for theatre actors, far too seriously and applied it in the practice of poetry-reading. The Nawab family of Bhopal hosted a dinner.

In 1982, we met again in Tokyo and Kyoto in the Asian Writers' Forum organised by the UNESCO. He had come straight from Beirut. He did not give any impression of his recalling our earlier meeting in Bhopal. In any case, in Bhopal, I did not speak much but kept on listening to him. But there was human warmth evident towards a younger Indian poet. We conversed mostly in Urdu-Hindi. In the first session of the Forum, he suddenly proposed that I should be made the permanent chairman of all the sessions. I was the youngest amongst the writers, who were participating in the Forum. When I showed some reluctance, he said that since I was young and had adequate knowledge of English, I would be better suited to control other oldies like him! Anyway, his proposal was accepted. The great Chinese poet I. Chhing was a participant along with an interpreter. Since the proceedings were in English, he used to listen quietly. When a Philipino writer mentioned Picasso in some context, he raised his hand to speak. Then, he launched upon a long narrative in Chinese, of his meeting Picasso, while in Paris. His intervention had nothing to do with the theme we were discussing. As the Chairman, I tried to stop him at which point, Faiz advised that an old Chinese writer was speaking in the Forum for the only time and he should be allowed to, even if what he was saying, was irrelevant.

The Forum used to have its sessions throughout the day and we used to return to the hotel rather exhausted. Invariably Faiz would ring me up in my room and we would spent long hours in the bar, chatting and drinking. It is then that I became aware of the vast span of his taste, knowledge and experience. He would readily laugh at himself. There was another writer from Pakistan who was a psychoanalyst and he would invariably be with us. Faiz would, sometimes publicly make statements which would be at vast variance from the official views of Pakistan and could even be turned against him. But the official representative of Pakistan did not dare to contradict him.

Every conference of UNESCO ends up in issuing a statement. At the suggestion of Faiz, it was resolved that I would prepare a draft statement for the Forum. The Japanese hosts were to bring a typewriter into my hotel room, for that purpose. When they came I was in the spirited company of Faiz and he instructed them to leave the typewriter in my room. We came out from the bar around 2 a.m., me cobbling, Faiz in good shape. I could not sleep due to nervousness and early in the morning, typed out the draft statement. Later, the Forum unanimously adopted it. During his stay in Japan, I could observe that Faiz listened carefully to others' opinions and remained remarkably alert in all circumstances.

Though Faiz was firmly rooted in Arabic-Persian tradition of Urdu, there are resonances in his poetry of the larger Indian tradition: *'Is tarah hai ki her ped koi mandir hai', 'De koi shankha duhai, koi payal bole/koi but jaage, koi sanvali ghunghat khole', 'Tore mandir me jo nahin aya', 'Aaj her sur se her ik raag ka naata tuta', 'kub se aas lagi darshan ki', 'Ik kunj ko sakhiyan chhor gayin aakash ki neeli rahon me', 'Ghat lagi her naav/raat gayi sukh jaga', 'Teri daya se deep jala hai is papan ke dware', 'Huth na karo man jao'.* A part of the poem by Faiz is as follows:

Vo Ishq ki ho ya jung ki ho

Gar Himmat hai to bismillah

Varna apne aap me raho
Lazim to nahin hai har koi
Mansur bane Farhad bane
Albatta itna lazim hai
Sach jaan ke jo bhi rah chune
Bas ek usi ka ho ke rahe

Faiz stuck to the path he chose. The universe of his poetry, kept on expanding. In spite of his romantic temperament, a lot more came within his poetic territory and he responded to important events and happenings, not only in Pakistan, but also in Europe, Africa, Vietnam etc.

He remained an alert and sympathetic poet. His claim, as given below, was genuine:

We are the sorrowful hearts of anguished mankind
A poet's temper is to battle
against injustice and tyranny;
We are the arbiters of good and evil,
right and wrong

If his voice is heard today with attention, it is because he is able to bring many anxieties and contradictions of our age into the realm of our living experience. The best poetry of Faiz was inspired and provoked by its time and therefore, carries scratches and wounds on its poetic body. But the real significance of it lies in the fact that these poems speak to us in our vastly and fast changing times and make us feel and see the romance and dreams of being human, the suffering and miseries, their dark interiors, which conceal light. It is a poetry which reassures us that it is possible to be human, to remain human in all circumstances. It seems so contemporary because of that pure core of humanness.

Christina Oesterheld*

Faiz the Internationalist

Keeping in mind Faiz's extraordinary popularity in India, Pakistan and among Urdu (and Hindi) speaking migrant populations all over the world, it is no wonder that much has been written about Faiz's political commitment, about his ideals, his poetics, his relation with classical Urdu poetry etc. Mujtaba Husain remarked, as early as 1965, that already every aspect of Faiz' works and personality has been discussed and it is difficult to think of anything to add.[1] His works have been translated into several languages, and in English alone, several versions of selected verses have been published by different translators. In view of this situation, the present presentation will be limited to a discussion of his contacts with the Soviet Union, setting off with his reminiscences, particularly about the Soviet Union, in Urdu prose which he wrote in 1974-75 at the request of Progress Publishers, Moscow, who published them in 1979 under the title 'Mah-o-sal-i ashnai' (Months and years of acquaintance). A Pakistani edition appeared in Karachi ('Maktabah-i Daniyal') in 1981.[2] The book consists of three parts: 1. Brief childhood memories and reports of Faiz's travels in the Soviet Union 2. Reports of meetings with eminent writers 3. Faiz's own poems and his translations of poems by others.

In the preface to his book, Faiz warns his readers not to expect a well-ordered, chronological narrative. Interestingly, he also adds the following

---

* Christina Oesterheld teaches Urdu at South Asia Institute, Department of Indology, University of Heidelberg, Heidelberg, Germany.

[1] Faiz - Muntakhab Mazamin, Islamabad: Muqtadara Qaumi Zaban, 2011, 78.

[2] Excerpts from the introduction to the book have been translated rather freely into English, by Khalid Hasan under the heading "Faiz Looks Back" in: 'Faiz Ahmad Faiz, O City of Lights: Selected Poetry and Biographical Notes.' Translations by Daud Kamal and Khalid Hasan. Sel. and ed. by Khalid Hasan: Karachi: OUP, 2006, pp. 58-63, corrsponding to pp. 7-12 of the Urdu original.

disclaimer: "Don't ask me anything other than stories about kindness and faithfulness!"

This is a very important statement, already foreboding what will be left out from his account, as we will see later. Going back to his early childhood memories, Faiz remembers the reverberations of the Russian revolution in his neighborhood. He recounts the gossip of common, illiterate labourers, small traders, butchers and barbers:

> "Within one year all the Englishmen, lords, commissioners, deputy commissioners will be thrown out and our own people will be put in their place." And: "My dear, I have heard that the forces of Gaazi Kamal Pasha have defeated the English and are advancing via Afghanistan."
>
> "Yes, yes, and the Russian forces have joined them. The Russian emperor Tsar has been de-throned, right? A new leader has appeared there, Lenin. He has prepared an army of workers, put the emperor to flight and distributed all money among the people." And: "He has established a workers' rule."

The tall hopes and naive expectations, expressed in these rumours are very similar to and as premature as, the main character's expectations in Manto's "Naya Qanoon". Faiz, then, goes on to mention, the growing militancy of the independence movement, the first acts of terrorism and the social unrest, due to deteriorating economic conditions.

Faiz continues his narrative with the story of his first contact with communists, his reading of the Communist Manifesto in 1935, which proved to be a revealing experience and led him to read many other communist writings, his meetings with eyewitnesses of the Russian revolution, and describes the dream of a New Adam, a new human being that the revolutionaries hoped to create. It is interesting that in the passages on the Second World War, he does not mention the deep crisis of the Indian Communist Party at the event of the Hitler-Stalin-Pact. This is his first, and obviously deliberate, major omission.

In 1949, he, for the first time, came into contact with a Soviet delegation that had arrived late for the conference of the Progressive Writers' Association, in Lahore. Again he met a Soviet delegation when he was allowed to take part in a conference of Asian writers in Delhi in 1956, where the Soviets tried their best to get African writers included into the movement. Here we come across an interesting statement, which partly explains why Faiz could stay on in Pakistan, at least most of the time:

> It was not long since I had been released from jail, but in the meantime the government had changed, and the new government included some persons kindly inclined towards me.

This sentence provides a clue to understanding how Faiz could survive and flourish in Pakistan (with the exception of the first years of Zia ul Haq's rule). He had already developed such a standing, had close personal relations with a number of influential persons and was so widely admired as a poet, even by many who did not share his ideals, that time and again, he was offered high positions in cultural institutions, sponsored by the administration. There can be no doubt that class solidarity often also cut across political affiliations, and Faiz, as many progressive Urdu poets and South Asian communists, came from a well-to-do, respected family, although Faiz had fallen on hard times after his father's death.

In 1958, Faiz, for the first time, visited the Soviet Union, together with Hafiz Jalandhari. Only these two had gotten the permission to attend. We need not forget that by this time, Pakistan had already joined the anti-Soviet cold war alliance CENTO (founded in 1954-55 by Iran, Iraq, Turkey, Pakistan and Great Britain, joined by the US in 1959). This visit was the beginning of a longstanding association between Faiz and the Soviet Union.

Faiz's report of what he saw in the Soviet Union, starting with his visit to Tashkent, now amounts to glimpses into a lost world. Thus he, for instance, describes the *Kolkhos* form of farms which had been created after expropriating feudal landowners and big farmers. He later visited Tashkent again after the devastating earthquake of 1967 and was impressed by the speed of reconstruction. He also relates the reports his hosts gave him of the economic success of their republic, without, however, ever voicing any doubt about their accuracy.

The next chapter deals with Samarkand and Bukhara. With regard to his travels in the Central Asian republics, Uzbekistan and Tajikistan, Faiz stressed the cultural similarities which made him feel at home, wherever he came. In Dushanbe (Tajikistan) Faiz was very happy to see that Sibli Nucmani's Shirul Ajam occupied a very prominent place in the great exhibition on the occasion of the one thousandth anniversary of Rudaki. He was astonished to find that here more people knew Iqbal's Persian poetry by heart than in South Asia. And wherever he went, Faiz was particularly impressed by the spread of education since the revolution. Faiz also was full of praise for the medical care provided to all citizens. He describes in detail how much care is taken of pregnant women and children right from their birth and the lung screening programme. Faiz obviously also had illusions about the end of social stratifications in a classless society (40-41). He was, however, right in noticing that hierarchies were less pronounced and there was a common form of address for everybody. Writing about Moscow, Faiz faithfully reports, that in 1958, the city was less busy and less colourful than other big cities in the West and that there still was a scarcity of many goods, whereas during later visits, he saw a lot of change, more goods in the shops, big department stores and lots of money to spend. (That not everybody had money to spare, he perhaps didn't know.) Turning to the multitude of nationalities and cultures within the Soviet Union, Faiz wonders how so many diverse cultural stages and traditions could be united into one common Soviet culture. He quotes Iqbal's concept of *khudi* in saying that after the revolution, many smaller nationalities, for the first time, came to realize their own selfhood (*khudi*) and to develop their own literature and culture. Thus, in a way, they have developed their cultural common market within the Union. Faiz probably thought of this Soviet version of "unity in diversity" also as a model for a multi-ethnic state such as Pakistan. He didn't live to see how this unity broke up as soon as the political pressure was gone. Faiz especially mentioned the common interest in cultural products cutting through all social classes and the great efforts made to acquaint children with all forms of culture. Following is a detailed report of his stay in Dagestan as guest of Rasul Hamza (Russian: Gamzatov), Maliku-Shuara of Dagistan, who was a member of the presiding committee of the Soviet parliament. There he met poets, doctors, engineers, university professors, members of the planning commission, and wondered what type of future career, parents, fifty or sixty years back, would have planned for their children: to send them to the army, teach them agriculture, at the utmost get them trained as *mullahs* in the local mosque or teachers in a primary school. He thus points out the new chances of social mobility opened up by Soviet rule.

Faiz felt the need to provide many details about the history and the present development because "our knowledge of the area is so meagre that it was necessary to mention some basic facts". Faiz was happy to note that in the Soviet Union in general and in the Muslim areas in particular, much respect was still shown to elders, whereas in the West, old age had become unfashionable and aged people tried their best to copy the young. To sum up the contents of this first part, one may say that Faiz devoted most of the space, to his travels in the Muslim territories of the Soviet Union. He obviously felt a close cultural affinity with the Central Asian people, based on a shared literary and religious heritage and common customs. But the second main aspect of these notes is his stress on the social achievements he noticed wherever he went in the Soviet Union: the spread of education and medical care, the industrial development of hitherto backward areas, the career opportunities for persons from all social strata, the representation of women in administration, educational institutions and in the economy, although he specifically mentioned the social practice of a certain degree of segregation in some Muslim territories. Faiz's conclusions about the reduction of social stratifications and hierarchies were perhaps too optimistic, but there can be no doubt that what he observed was far removed from realities in South Asia. Taken as a whole, it seems that many of his dreams about a brighter future, social justice, enlightenment and welfare of the people appeared to have come true in the Soviet Union.

In addition to this internal factor, Faiz profited from and contributed to the international cultural activities of the Soviets, which can more cynically be attributed to the Cold War, but in their essence were part of an internationalist socialist ethos of anti-colonialism and anti-imperialism, which aimed at freedom from all kinds of oppression and exploitation and world peace. Soviet publishing houses commissioned translations from all the major languages of the world into Russian and from Russian into numerous languages, particularly of the third World. A part of it no doubt consisted of the classics of Marxism and Leninism and of propaganda literature, but these programmes also included major classics of world literature and many authors from Asian, African and Latin American countries. In a way these efforts, of which Faiz became an active part through his editorial work with *Lotus* and through his translations, were a continuation of the now, much maligned enlightenment project and the project of modernity. The disenchantment with socialist ideas brought about by the Stalin terror, by events such as the suppression of the Hungarian and Czeck uprisings and the Soviet invasion in Afghanistan and the final collapse of the Soviet block have largely obliterated the legitimacy of the ideals as such. For Faiz, however, the social achievements of the socialist countries still held much appeal, especially in view of the failure to build just and equitable societies on the Subcontinent. This may serve to explain why Faiz does not mention any of the grim aspects of Soviet history, especially the atrocities committed in the Stalin period. He perhaps did not see, or didn't want to see the inner contradictions of the Soviet system which would finally cause its collapse: the lack of freedom, the official hypocrisy and make-believe, but most importantly the economic failure of a system, which failed to take into account, human greed and selfishness. The New Man did not emerge after all, and probably never will. To sum up, in his relation with the Soviet Union, as in other regards, Faiz made certain compromises. He kept mum on questions which could have annoyed his Soviet counterparts. The Soviet authorities always did their best to let their guests see only the sunny side of things, and Faiz perhaps chose to ignore aspects of life in the Soviet Union, which ran counter to his vision of a free and just socialist society, although he made a strong statement for freedom, in his speech, on the occasion of being awarded the Lenin Peace Price in 1962.[3] But even then, here at least, parts of his dreams and ideals were realised, and the Soviet Union was the strongest bulwark against Western imperialism and exploitation. Hence Faiz had many good

---

[3] An Urdu version of the speech is included in Faiz - Muntaxab Mazaamin, Islamabad: Muqtadara Qaumi Zaban, 2011, pp. 633-636. Here he not only speaks of freedom from colonial oppression and exploitation, but also of freedom within society.

reasons to remain loyal to his Soviet friends. Despite all obvious omissions, his reminiscences and observations are not only an important personal, but also a valuable historical document. They allow glimpses into the spirit of the decades between the late thirties and the early seventies, written by an eyewitness who was actively involved in the cultural politics of Third World solidarity. From the literary point of view, however, the second and third parts are more important. Here he not only speaks of freedom from colonial oppression and exploitation, but also of freedom within society.

In his introduction to the second part titled "Mukalama" Faiz writes:

> Moscow is like an international guesthouse for writers and intellectuals from all over the world. Someone came for one day, another for a month, and somebody like the deceased Turkish poet Nazim Hikmet came never to leave again. Hence, for merely mentioning the names of all the eminent personalities whom I met in Moscow and other cities of the Soviet Union I would need a whole register book (daftar).

He mentions Italy's Alberto Moravia, Jean Paul Sartre, Prof. Empson, Angus Wilson and William Golding from England, Africa's Leopold Singhure, Pablo Neruda from Latin America, several Arab authors and then recollects his meetings with Nazim Hikmet, Ilja Ehrenburg, Jean Paul Sartre, Umar Ali Sulaimanow (Kazakh writer) and Chingiz Aitmatow (Kirghiz writer). Faiz claims to have a very bad memory, hence reports only bits and pieces he remembers, of his conversations. One of the most fruitful encounters seems to have been that with Nazim Hikmet (1902-1963), the most famous Turkish poet of the twentieth century. His poems, which were banned in Turkey had been published first in Bulgaria in 1954, and translations of his works subsequently appeared there and in Greece, Germany, Italy, and the USSR. He died of a heart attack in Moscow in June 1963. Faiz had read a slim volume of his poetry in English translation, in Lahore. It consisted mainly of prison poems. When he escaped from prison, he got asylum in the Soviet Union but despite leading a comfortable life there, his heart always longed for his home, which turned most of his poems into sad elegies. For the Afro-Asian Writers Conference at Tashkent in 1958, a *mushaira* had been organised which was a new thing for most of the participants. Here Faiz met Nazim Hikmet for the first time. They became friends and remained friends until Hikmet's sudden death in 1963. His dramas had been played in Moscow and many other cities. Faiz had long discussions with him about poetics, style, language usage etc. Nazim Hikmet rejected the concept that poetry could only be created in the traditional patterns and forms. He believed in the poetic potential of colloquial language. The poet should try to discover the natural rhythm and melodiousness of the spoken language and bring his poetry as close as possible to it. He specifically criticised the custom to follow Arabic prosody in languages such as Urdu or Turkish. Nazim Hikmet tried to free himself from the fetters of Arabic prosody and thus arrived at a new rhythm and at free verse. In this, he was later followed by many modern Turkish poets. Faiz mentions that several poems he wrote in Moscow and which are included in the present collection are a result of these discussions with Nazim Hikmet. It is certainly no coincidence that free poems start to appear in Faiz's collections for the first time in 1962/63 *(Jab teri samundar aankhon mein in* 'Dast-i tah-i sang', 1965, also included in *Mah-o-sal)* after interaction with Nazim Hikmet and Pablo Neruda. Thus, Faiz states that his poems 'Rang hai dil ka mere', 'Ahista' and some others 'reflect Nazim Hikmet' *(...me Nazim Hikmet ka aks hai)*. Faiz reports Hikmet as saying that he thought his earliest poetry which was predominantly political and used in mass meetings and rallies, was one-dimensional and could fulfil short term needs, but its language and diction did not reflect the depth and intricacy of human experience. Faiz certainly attributed great importance to this statement since the aesthetic aspect of works of literature, was in the centre of many discussions on progressive writing, and going by Faiz's own works, one can safely assume that he fully agreed with Nazim Hikmet. Hikmet also stressed the inseparableness of tradition, form and subject. When it was suited to the material, he also used strict formal patterns, local language or expressions of the past. He compares the form to a silk stocking on a beautiful woman's white leg/shank - it should enhance the leg's beauty but should itself not be too visible. Occasionally, Hikmet also recited some verses. Faiz has included some translations, although he feels of the fact, that they can hardly convey the beauty of the original. The third part consists of poems and translations (Rasul Gamzatow, Oljaz Umar

Ali Sulaimanow, Nazim Hikmet). Faiz reports that from his journeys, he usually brought back some verses. Why? Because outside his usual surroundings, he had more leisure to write and less distractions. In the Soviet Union, he was relieved from his daily worries and concerns and despite all activities, found enough time to concentrate on poetry:

> ... aur is fursat ke sath sath gham-e-daura aur gham-e-jana dono se vah duri aur fasla bhi aa hi jate hai ki admi ek tamashaee ki tarah un ko sukun se nazara kar sake. Sher likhne ke liye ghaliban mahsusat ki dunya se qurb aur duri, rabt aur alhidagi, fikr aur sarkhushi (involvement aur detachment) dono zaroori hai. aur vah kaifiyat bhi jise sufiya ke istilah me 'insirah-i qalb' kahte hai. jab yun mahsoos hota hai ki apne aur husn-i alam ke darmiyan ghair az nigah ab koi hail nahi rahi.

This mood, he attained occasionally in Moscow, Ashkabad or Leningrad. In the poems included here, there is no mention of Moscow, but the mood was present everywhere. The most important factor was the company of Soviet and international writers which also served as an impetus and inspiration and provided new perspectives' patterns of writing. The poem 'Intisab', for instance, was written over a span of several months, partly in Moscow, partly in Sochi, inspired by Pablo Neruda. With Rasul Hamza's poetry, he got so close that he translated several of his verses in one sitting, which are included in the volume.

As far as Nazim Hikmet's poetry is concerned, Intizar Husain reports in an article on English translations by Masud Akhtar Sheikh: "Sheikh talks of his contacts with Faiz Sahib during his last years and 'his intense desire to translate Nazim Hikmet into Urdu.' Faiz had to acquaint himself with the original text of the poems he intended to translate, but unfortunately he did not live long enough to do what he had dreamt." However, as far as the end result is concerned, Faiz's translations are very beautiful poems in their own right. Look at the following examples:

Veerra Ke Naam

Us ne kaha aao
phir usne kaha thahro
muskao kaha usne
mar jao kaha usne
main aya,
main thahar gaya
muskaya
aur mar bhi gaya

Or compare the following English translation of a part from Nazim Hikmet's "Letters from Prison" by Randy Blasing and Mutlu Konuk with Faiz's version:

Sunday today.
Today they took me out in the sun for the first time.
And I just stood there, struck for the first time in my life
by how far away the sky is,
how blue
and how wide.
Then I respectfully sat down on the earth.
I leaned back against the wall.
For a moment no trap to fall into,
no struggle, no freedom, no wife.
Only earth, sun, and me...
I am happy.

Aaj peer ka din hai
aur aaj pehli baar
voh mujhe baahar khuli hawa mein le kar gaye

aaj zindagi mein pehli baar
main ne hairat se dekha
ki aasman kitna neela hai
aur kitna dur
main dhoop mein sakat khada raha
aur phir adab se sar jhuka kar
patthar ki deewar se tek laga kar
baith gaya
aur phir yakbargi sab kuchh bhool gaya
khwabein bhi
azaadi bhi
aur tum bhi meri jaan
bas ek suraj, dharti aur main
uff kitna sukh hai, kitna sukh hai

Faiz's poetic diction was enriched by his vast reading and by his translation activities, and he also served as a poetic bridge between South Asia and the world. In this regard, his interaction with Nazim Hikmet seems to have been of utmost importance. Both poets shared not only ideals, but also many personal experiences and aesthetic concerns. Both were great humanists, both despite all repression, loved their country, and both loved life and its beauty. Especially the poems Faiz wrote during his stays in the Soviet Union and in Beirut, clearly bear the stamp of his exposure to the writings of Nazim Hikmet and, perhaps to a lesser degree, other contemporary poets. The poem Faiz wrote for Nazim Hikmet, beautifully sums up their attitude to life:

jeene ke liye marna
kaisi saadat hai
aur marne ke liye jina
yeh kaisi himaqat hai

akele jiyo

ek shamshad tan ki tarah
aur mil kar jiyo
ek ban ki tarah

hamne umeed ke sahare
tut kar yun hi zindagi ki hai
jis tarah tum se ashiqi ki hai

There can be no doubt that Faiz's main achievement is his poetry, but his prose writings have a value of their own, as documents of a crucial period in history, of which he not only was an eyewitness but also an important agent and as insights into his aesthetic concerns.

Kedar Nath Singh*

I have seen Faiz

Faiz has been talked about so often that discussing his poetry seems reiterating the same, again and again. I had the occasion to watch and listen to him, from close quarters, so I will talk only about that.

I first heard of Faiz when I was an Intermediate student. Today I can recall the couplet of Faiz which I first heard and got introduced to him. It was an old romantic one :

> My hopes do not diminish
> Whether I go to him or not.

I had stopped at these last lines and they are still fresh in my memory. But that was not the real Faiz. Romanticism is surely a part of his whole make-up, but the true identity of Faiz, shaped up gradually on the basis of his various other revolutionary *ghazals* and *nazms* that left indelible impression on the minds of numerous young readers, like me. Here I would like to share another incident. One fine day (I was perhaps in B.A. final year or M.A. Previous) I got a printed card from Sachchidanand Hiranand Vaatsyayan 'Agyeya' informing me about an Asian Writers' Conference. The venue was Delhi and many big names of Asian literature were coming. I fondly remember that I had gone all the way to see the conference with some other writers of Benaras. I am deliberately using the word 'see' because a young writer like me could only see such a mega literary event. There, I saw Faiz Ahmed Faiz, along with others. I still remember how the stage looked and who were sitting there: there were Rahul Sankrityayan, Laxmi Prasad Devkota and Faiz. I also remember how the hall kept reverberating

---

* Kedar Nath Singh is a celebrated Hindi poet, a former Professor, School of Language, Literature and Culture Studies, Jawaharlal Nehru University (JNU), New Delhi.

with the sound of clapping, when the presenter mentioned his presence. This was the first time when I saw Faiz, live. The conference was being held in Vigyan Bhavan and I was sitting in the last row and what I remember most vividly from whatever my young eyes could see from there, was his remarkable silence that reminded me of his famous couplet :

> My silence echoed in such a way
>
> As if replies came from all directions

I had only this much of a remote connection with him, but this hazy remembrance worked for me like a lost treasure in 1978. I had joined JNU (Jawaharlal Nehru University) by then and I had gone to watch the famous play 'Begum Ka Takiya' in Meghdoot auditorium with some friends. There, at the end of the front row, I saw a face that vaguely resembled the face that my young eyes had seen in Vigyan Bhavan. As the play ended, some of us rushed towards the person who resembled Faiz and who was briskly pacing ahead. As I reached closer, I could not hold my curiosity and at once asked, ' Excuse me ! Are you Faiz Ahmed Faiz ?' He was surprised for a moment and in a muffled voice mumbled 'yes'. Later, I came to know that he had secretly come to India and did not want that media should come to know of it. However, while departing, some of my friends and I, requested him to visit JNU someday. He nodded in agreement.

Faiz came to JNU, after a prolonged wait. I must mention here that it was DP Tripathi's (the legendary student leader) intimacy with Faiz that eventually worked and Faiz came to JNU. I have been in JNU for nearly 24 years but what I saw that day was totally unprecedented. His arrival was a huge celebration - it was like a minor movement in which almost the entire Delhi was participating. Such was the multitude that the last and the tallest person who stood far behind at the end of the crowd was none other than Maqbul Fida Hussain. He was as usual bare feet. It was pure charm of Faiz that had drawn such a huge crowd there. I do not exactly remember what Faiz said at that occasion. He was not a good orator. I do remember that he had recited some *ghazals* and he recited them so plainly that it seemed as if he was not enjoying them at all. After repeated requests, he recited only those few *ghazals* which he wanted to recite and then became silent. His visit to India, after such a long time was a big event in the cultural history of India and it was widely reported in the newspapers.

I can recollect another two small incidents. Once, we went to meet Faiz in his hotel. I do not exactly remember what the name of the hotel was. I was with Namvar Singh and perhaps there was someone else also. We saw Faiz sitting alone in the room, facing the wall. On a small stool beside him, a filled up glass with some ice cubes, was placed. The scene appeared strange to me. I could not control myself and asked abruptly: "Faiz Sahab, why are you drinking facing the wall?" He laughed and replied, "This is a good question. One should never drink alone."

That was an ironic comment on the loneliness and deep seated agony of a renowned poet. My last meeting with Faiz took place at the house of Sheela Sandhu. A large number of people had been invited and the gathering included Dr. Karan Singh and the then High Commissioner of Pakistan, Mr. Abdul Sattar. Many other Hindi writers were also present there. I particularly remember two or three things.

Dr. Karan Singh recited several poems of Faiz directly from his memory and in the end, sang some Dogri folk songs too. I did not know that he could sing so well. Faiz mostly read *nazms.* While reciting a *ghazal,* he got stuck at one point and suddenly somebody from behind prompted him - he took the cue and recollected the lost line. The man who prompted him was Pakistan's High Commissioner. Faiz looked at him once and continued reading. He did not pay any more attention. However, as Faiz stopped, the High Commissioner rushed to him and after exchanging pleasantries stood in front of him. Faiz gestured for him to sit down but he remained standing and kept talking to him for some time before moving off and finding a seat somewhere in the back rows. The last part of this incident is related to that *nazm* which is one of my favourite poems of Faiz. The poem is titled 'Raqib Se' i.e. 'To the Rival in Love'. I had also read Firaq Gorakhpuri's famous article on that poem. Apparently, the word 'Raqib' has an orthodox meaning in Urdu tradition and the biggest achievement of the poem lies, in the fact, that it fills this commonplace symbol with a whole new human dimension. And it is in this sense that this poem occupies a historic place in the world of love poems. When Faiz had read several of his *ghazals and nazms,* I requested him to recite 'Raqib Se'. He said, "No, I won't. There are things which flow out of your tongue, hang in the air for sometime and then fall flat on your head. This is one of those *nazms.*" Still when many people pressed for that, he relented and recited the *nazm* but stopped when he reached the following couplet :

> What I have lost and what I have learnt in your love
>
> I cannot explain to anyone else except you

Even after repeated requests he did not recite the poem any further, and whispered, "the *nazm* ends here." There are 14 more lines in that *nazm* which are a bit loud and they were on the lines of the progressive thinking, prevalent during those times. Faiz considered the latter part unnecessary and so did not recite them. This was introspection as well as his own understanding of art as a great poet. Faiz had this moral courage in him and he also had his own inimitable style of expressing it.

Atul Tiwari*

Lucknow of Faiz Ahmed Faiz

This paper was especially written and presented at the colloquium on Faiz, at his centenary celebrations at Lahore on the 12th February, 2011 - Editor.

Honourable Guests!

This gathering will mark a memorable date in the history of our literature. In our conferences and colloquiums, we have been mostly arguing about the language and its spread/power. So much so, that the intention of early Hindi and Urdu Literature - which is present - was not to impact our thoughts and emotions, but to make a perfect linguistic construct.

But language is but a bridge and not the destination. Literature has been defined in various ways, but in my opinion, the most apt definition of literature is - "A critique of our life and our world" - be it in the form of essays, stories or poetry. It must analyse and critique our life.

The era that we have been through had no imagination about literature being connected with real life. The measure of love was titillation of senses and the ideal of beauty was to satiate the eyes. The job of poetry was to work towards these sensory emotions. And we all know how popular such poetry is even today.

Can a literature, that makes us escape the real world and its problems, ever fulfil our mental and emotional needs? Carnality is only a part of our being, and if that is the chief concern of a body of literature, then it cannot be the pride of a people in their society. A writing that does not incite true commitment and a conviction to overcome our problems - is useless for us today! 'Progressive Writers' Association'. The idea of a Progressive Writer, in my opinion, is a fallacy. A writer or an artist, by his very nature, is progressive. Had that not been the nature, he or she might not have been a writer at all.

---

* Atul Tiwari is a distinguished film maker based in Mumbai.

We will have to change the scales by which we measure Beauty. Literature (till today) did not accept that 'hunger and nudity' could also be aesthetic. It saw beauty in an attractive young lady but not in the poor unattractive mother, who puts her child to sleep in the field, as she sweats in heat. Literature has decided that beauty lies in the painted lips, soft cheeks and arched eyebrows and not in the mangled hair, dry chapping lips and withered cheeks! But that is the offence of its narrow vision.

When we refuse to tolerate a system that makes thousands slave under a brute force, then our self-esteem would goad us to raise a flag of revolt against this capitalistic, dictatorial, militaristic culture. Only then, writing quietly on a piece of paper would not suffice.

A Litterateur's mission is not simply to assemble gatherings and to entertain. Let's not degrade him so much. Literature is not even meant to succumb to patriotism and politics. It is a torch which marches ahead, illuminating their paths.

Until the time Literature's function was only producing mere mindless amusement, singing lullabies or shedding tears - we did not need a new practice & protocol for it. It was a lunatic-romantic whose grief fed others' appetite for amusement. But we don't consider Literature as a mere thing of entertainment, amusement and appeasement of senses. On our new measure, literature is that, which has exalted thoughts, passion for freedom, aesthetic for beauty, constructive spirit, and that throws light on the reality of life. Literature is that which incites, inspires, inconveniences and invigorates us and not that which lulls us to sleep. For now, to sleep is to die."

Friends, of course, these are neither my words nor my expression. I wish I could ever be as lucid, insightful, in-depth and intense. What you just read here was a gurbaani/kalma/gayatrimantra/holy invocation which, in a ritual of initiation, was whispered into the ears of Faiz by a man called Dhanpat Rai. The date was: 10th of April 1936, and the place: the city of Lucknow. This inaugural address, delivered by Munshi Premchand, at the first conference of the PWA, was going to be a watershed moment, which would change the scenario of literature, arts, theatre, films and even politics in India. And it was no coincidence that Faiz, who had travelled all the way from Punjab, was present in Lucknow, that evening. Faiz, who had just turned 25, was young and full of verve, impressive and impressionable. And the stamp/imprint that Lucknow left on him, the bond that this city made with him was the bedrock of a life-long relationship.

Actually, the foundation of his bond with Lucknow was laid the day Dr. Rasheed Jahan settled down in Lucknow, after leaving Amritsar. And who, amongst you, is not aware of the name and personality of Dr. Rasheed Jahan - a novelist, short story writer, dramatist, doctor and most of all a committed comrade? *"Angaarey"(Embers)*, the collection of Short Stories written by Sajjad Zaheer, Mahmood-uz-Zafar, Rashid Jahan and Ahmad Ali and published in 1932, was a trail blazer that had scorched people all over the country. And when the British banned the book, in 1933, Dr. Rasheed became famous, even in circles where one had not heard her name. Her husband, the learned communist Com. Mahmood-uz-Zafar, was the principal of MAO College, Lahore. It was during his tenure that Faiz, a fresh post-graduate of English & Arabic, was appointed a lecturer there. Dr. Rasheed Jahan and Com. Mahmood-uz-Zafar were also the first ones to have introduced Faiz to the progressive revolutionary thoughts and tenets of Marxism. With such a mentor being in Lucknow, Faiz, probably, would have been looking forward to come to Lucknow anyway. And the first conference of Progressive Writers' Association (PWA) pulled him with such intensity that, with only a one way fare in his pocket, Faiz left for Lucknow. PWA's first conference was conceived-convened-catered-cared for by Hon'ble Sajjad Zaheer Sahib. Faiz had been introduced to him, earlier in Amritsar, by Dr. Rasheed Jahan. But at Sajjad Zaheer's home ground, Lucknow, Faiz was even more impressed - rather besotted - by his magnetic persona. After the PWA conference, with the return fare realised from Dr. Rasheed Jahan, Faiz somehow returned to Lahore. But not before a deep bond had been formed between Faiz & Lucknow. And since then, whenever he got a chance, Faiz eagerly waited to go to Lucknow and Lucknow always awaited him.

The Lucknow of those days was not just another township. It was the conurbation of Anwar Jamal Kidwai, Sibte Hasan, Farahtullah Ansari, Ali Jawad Zaidi, Yashpal, Dr. Ashraf, Dr. Z. A. Ahmed and his wife Hajra Aapa. This was the urbane capital of Awadh where Journals and Newspapers like *'National Herald', 'The Pioneer', 'Hindustan', 'Viplav', and 'Naya-Adab'* were published. Along with that, the hospitable home of the Vice Chancellor of Lucknow University, Mr. Sheikh Habibullah, and the personal library of Prof. D.P. Mukherjee, were places where young writers thronged. No less famous were the coffee-house, restaurants and bars of Hazratganj, along with tea-houses, bookshops of Ameenabad, and the Qahwa-kiosks of the Chowk. In Dec 1941, Faiz once again got to travel to Lucknow, 'officially', when Somnath Chhib, the director of All India Radio, invited him to present his poems at the symposium of young emerging poets. Veteran poet Josh Malihabadi was invited too - not to recite his work - but to listen to the young poets and chair the event. Of course, amongst other aficionados, Faiz's friend Sajjad Zaheer was present with his wife Razia, to listen to the young voices. And those voices consisted of almost the whole catalogue of Progressive poets like Majaz, Jazbi, Jaan Nisaar Akhtar, Ali Sardar Jafri and Faiz Ahmed Faiz.

The presence of Sajjad Zaheer, recently released from colonial jail, added a new enthusiasm, a new experience, a new verve and a new commitment to the voices of young poets. To say that the symposium was a runaway success is not important. But on that cold December night, the sheer energy and warmth that the company of these young fellow-travellers, comrades-in-arms generated is worth listening to, in words of Ali Sardar Jafri:

"That little house, located in Kandhari Lane, had a small bench, a few cane stools and three cots in the name of furniture. We pushed all that aside into a corner and covered the whole floor with mats. Above the mantelpiece was a big portrait of a Spanish revolutionary girl - her fists clinched, and breast protruding in a way, that even the military-uniform failed to conceal the curves. Below the portrait it was written, "To Death". The flickering light of candles - perched on two inverted buckets made this portrait even livelier, inspiring and touching...The warmth of our little congress, the intoxication of hearts and the glow of faces kept increasing by the minute. Praises were being showered as if lovers were complimenting each other. Just then Faiz said, "I heard this wonderful couplet in Lahore, though I don't know the name of the poet." And he quoted:

> When the boat was new, solid, intact, who wished to see the shore,
>
> Now with boat all tattered-shattered, who would dream to come ashore

Jazbi's melancholic face just lit up. It was his couplet that had travelled all the way from Lucknow to Lahore and back. Faiz and Jazbi hugged each other. And when Faiz was just about to sit, Jazbi, without any invitation, started reciting Faiz's 'Mauzu-e-Sukhan', in tune:

The melancholic aflame evening will melt soon

And night will emerge, bathed in the brook of moon

Now you will hear from the eager eyes beautiful and bold

And feel the touch of hands that you wanted to hold

Jazbi sang the first stanza and Majaz followed with the second - in his own peculiar style. And then both, alternately, kept reciting stanzas from Faiz's long poem. Faiz's face lit with a smile of innocence and contentment. There could not have been a better compliment for a poet. And probably this was possible only in Lucknow. This night left such a lasting impression on Faiz that, 12 years later, in a letter written to his dear *bhabhi* (sister-in-law) Razia, he reminisces about this night. After the next year, the situation in the country and the world started changing dramatically and at a break-neck pace with World War II, Quit India, Do or Die, Freedom and Partition or Partition and Freedom. But even amidst all this chaos, Faiz stayed connected with Lucknow, through his friend-philosopher-guide, Sajjad Zaheer.

Even though new lines had been drawn on the map of the world and now two nations had become a reality of our sub-continent, still some people refused to accept this and their slogan was:

With hunger poor still die, such a 'freedom' is a lie

Among those were Faiz and his friend, fellow and 'elder brother' Sajjad Zaheer, who was sent from India to re-establish the communist movement in the newly made Pakistan. It had not even been 4 years since freedom that Faiz and Sajjad Zaheer were both arrested and incarcerated again, in 1951. For the next 4 years, these brothers-in-arms were forced to spent countless time in innumerable jails, facing limitless hardships, immeasurable suffering and indescribable torture. They were both subjected to solitary confinement as well. When one thinks about this period one wonders, what would have happened if this man from Lahore was not accompanied by the man from Lucknow, in the confines of gaol. And probably without this forced confluence of Awadh and Punjab in prison, a whole body of Faiz's work, that emerged from the dark depths of detention, may not have emerged at all.

During this period, on 22nd May 1952, Faiz, in a reply to a letter by Razia Sajjad Zaheer, writes "You asked me, if I have seen Lucknow or not? I sure have seen it, but I lust for it even more. I have been to Lucknow a few times - stayed for 2-3 days at your house too - but could never stay beyond a couple of days. Each time, instead of coming back contented, I have come back yearning for more."

After being released from the Pakistani jail, Sajjad Zaheer returned back to India. But both the friends continued frequenting jails in their respective countries. Since then, whenever Faiz came to Lucknow, he always visited Sajjad & Razia Zaheer at their house on Wazir Hasan Road. Sajjad Zaheer's four daughters were for Faiz, like his own daughters. The depth of the bonding between these two greats of this era can perhaps be understood by the lines that Faiz uttered when Sajjad Zaheer suddenly passed away:

Take the cups away, the bottle, and the wine-measure

Close this evening soiree for ever

Just raise a toast of farewell to the departed friend

Then smash the wine-glass, bringing this party to an eternal end

With Sajjad Zaheer's passing away, a strong connection between Faiz and Lucknow was broken, but there were many others threads through which Lucknow had tied him to itself. One such connect was through a voice. The voice of Begum Akhtar. From the beginning of Faiz's career till the end, the way Begum Akhtar understood, interpreted and rendered Faiz's poetry in her inimitable voice, is legendary. This osmotic relationship between word and voice had taken both these artists to new unconquered heights. And whenever Faiz visited Lucknow, he did make it a point to visit Begum Akhtar at her 4, Finebrake Avenue home. Sometimes, on such tours Faiz had to be subjected to very ingenious Lucknow humour too. A few of Faiz's fans once took him to Abdullah Hotel in Ameenabad, which was a known hotspot for tea, Qahwa and lively gatherings of poets. When Faiz reached there, all the litterateurs stood up as a mark of respect to him, except one. His name was Nazir Khayyam. Somebody asked him "Nazir Sahab, would you not show any courtesy towards such a senior poet?" To which he replied, "I don't consider Faiz to be a poet at all." When asked why, he retorted, "Faiz has written in a poem:

> Having loved and lost both the worlds to her,
>
> He walks away after spending a night of despair

"He must explain", demanded Khayyam, "whether the two worlds that he lost in love, were his to begin with, did his father bequeath them to him that he was so careless about them? And when there are only two worlds in this whole cosmos, where does he reside right now, after having lost both of them?" Faiz himself, could not but laugh at this wit and repartee and conceded the point. And Mr. Khayyam immediately stood and saluted him with all respect due to a senior poet. The connects, between Faiz and Lucknow, that I have mentioned till now have been written, noted and talked about by others too. But there was another deep rooted relationship that Faiz had, with the city of Lucknow. And this one lived in a narrow unsung lane of Khayaliganj, right behind the Police Station of Kaiserbagh. This man was neither a poet, nor an intellectual, or even a political ideologue. This man was just a common committed foot soldier of the communist party. But the bond of this relationship was so strong that once in 70's, when Faiz came to Lucknow and checked into the first Five-Star Hotel in Lucknow - Clarks Awadh, he immediately asked his hosts, "I have a friend who lives in Lucknow now. Could you get me the number of the office of Communist Party of India here, so I could enquire about him? "When the phone got connected to the CPI's office, Faiz asked, "Could I speak to Naeem Khan?" Incidentally it was Naeem Khan on the other side because he was the office secretary of CPI. "Yes, Comrade! It's Naeem here.""Naeem, this is Faiz..." The voices choked and tear began to flow silently. Actually, Comrade Naeem as a foot soldier of the party, had been sent to Lahore at one point of time. There, the relationship that developed between Faiz and Naeem Khan was something like a bond between a deity and a devotee. It was mutual admiration. And when Faiz left Lahore, to go to Srinagar to wed Alys, Comrade Naeem accompanied him with the wedding party, consisting of barely a couple of other friends. Sheikh Abdullah solemnized this Nikah-marriage in the palace of Maharaja Hari Singh and Com. Naeem along with Gul Jafri and Noor Hassan, signed the *nikah-nama* as a witness.

Immediately after the phone call, Com. Naeem reached Faiz's hotel, stepping into a five-star environs perhaps for the first time in his life. Two old friends met and hugged each other as if this was the moment they had been living for. "Faiz you should come home!" "Let's go." "But my house is in a very narrow lane...""So what?" Passing through the narrow lanes and by lanes of Khayaliganj, when Faiz reached Com. Naeem's house, it was already full of people from the neighborhood and other party comrades. An eye witness of this evening Shakeel Siddiqui writes:

> Both the friends had tears in their eyes and a vision which could see far beyond. Faiz enquired about the welfare of other members of the family, greeted all the gathered guests, lit up a cigarette and silently sat down in a corner. Comrade Naeem exerted his right, 'Bhai Faiz, recite something for us. ''What?" "Anything". And Faiz began reciting in his inimitable style and the audience was mesmerized. The evening was still unfolding when a young girl asked Faiz, 'Uncle, you must sing that one..., you know. "Which one?" The one that you wrote in the jail ."Oh! I wrote so many in the jail, after all this was the biggest advantage of going to the jail'. Everybody laughed out aloud but for the girl...

Friends, two days before leaving for Lahore, to attend Faiz's centenary celebrations there, I went to meet Late Comrade Naeem's wife, Shameema, and son Asad. Aunt Shameema, without who's sweet-sewaiyyans my Eid would never feel like one, is now very old, and has almost lost her memory. But as soon as I mentioned Faiz, her eyes lit up. She started reminiscing how her son Bablu had asked uncle Faiz if he had written songs for films too. Faiz had replied in affirmative. Then Bablu asked him to sing one film song, but Faiz deferred the request saying, "I don't remember any right now". But Bablu, meaning Asad, was not embarrassed by his childhood antic that evening; on the contrary he was proud of his little exchange with, arguably, the greatest Urdu poet of 20th century. Asad told me that when some one asked Faiz to, "sing" one of his poems, he dismissed him, saying, "Singing is the work of crooners and dancers, not of poets." But when Comrade Karnal Singh, a Sikh refugee from Punjab, requested him to recite some Punjabi poems, Faiz had immediately obliged. The last long association between Faiz and Lucknow happened in 1981, when, like in the rest of the world, Lucknow too celebrated the 70th birthday of Faiz. The elegant event was hosted in the historical Safed Baradari, a favourite venue for the pomp of last Awadh Nawab Wajid Ali Shah. The then Mayor of Lucknow, Dr. Dauji Gupta recollected that 30 year old evening as if it happened just yesterday. He told me enthusiastically, "Once you are back from Lahore, we will also celebrate a Faiz Centenary here, like we celebrated his 70 years."

As I got up from the coffee-house at Hazratganj to leave, I was wondering that 2011 is a year of centenary celebrations in India, as poets Shamsher, Agyeya, Nagarjun, Kedarnath and Majaz are all completing their hundred years. But is there a poet whose centenary celebrations will happen with such intensity, enthusiasm and fervour, not only on both sides of the borders, but in the whole world, as Faiz's Centenary Celebrations? The answer is clear. And why not! Amongst all the names that I just listed, Faiz was the only poet-man-comrade whose sphere was not limited by any geographical, cultural or national boundaries. He belonged as much to Asia as to Africa, as much to Beirut as to Bangladesh, as much to Pakistan as to India, and belonged as much to Lahore as he belonged to Lucknow. I am very grateful to Faiz's daughters Salima and Moneeza, who not only have been celebrating Faiz with mass melas every year, but have now made a befitting museum to him called 'Faiz Ghar'. His centenary celebrations have brought Faiz's scholars and fans, like me, from all over the world to Faiz's Lahore. For such passion, Faiz's Lucknow salutes Faiz's Lahore. Long live Lahore. Long live Lucknow. Long live Faiz!

Raihan Raza*

A close reading of select poems by Faiz Ahmed Faiz

In his book "The Auden Generation" Samuel Hynes opines:

> A close relation exists between literature and history, and I think that this relation is particularly close in times of crisis, when public and private lives, the world of action and the world of imagination, interpenetrate. I do not believe that literary history can be separated from social and political and economic history . . .'

This is applicable to Faiz Ahmed Faiz in undivided India, in much the same way as to the Auden generation in England, in the early part of the 20th century. The period is marked by struggle and strife, upheaval and turmoil. The poetry of Faiz Ahmed Faiz is firmly rooted in the major events and pre-occupations of the times in which he lived. A study of his poetry reveals that it records as well as creates the consciousness of his countrymen to quite an extent. In his works, there is often a simmering resentment which flowers into full fledged revolt against colonial rule and oppression which he verbalises without mincing words. Faiz was also deeply moved by the sufferings of common people and fervently wished to improve their lot. He was drawn to Communism as opposed to both Fascism and Capitalism, realising that the condition of the disadvantaged sections of humanity could improve under a socialist ideology.

Faiz wanted to usher in a world order based on the principles of justice and equality, humanism and brotherhood as is made clear by poems such as 'The Morning of Freedom, August 1947', 'Blackout', 'The Festival of

---

* Raihan Raza is an Associate Professor, Department of English, Aligarh Muslim University, Aligarh.

Bloodshed' and 'The Dust of Hatred in My Eyes'. Faiz also sings of hope for the hopeless, freedom, in spite of being held in chains, as poems such as 'Hold on Restless Heart' bear witness. His was a wide canvas, not limited to the state of his own country and its inhabitants. Poems such as 'We Who Were Slain in Unlit Pathways' testify to this assertion.

This paper with the help of a close reading of select poems, highlights the note of protest that runs through most of his greatest texts. The text that I have largely used for the purpose of my study is the English translation by Shiv K. Kumar, entitled 'The Best of Faiz'.

Most of the time, poets writing poetry in Urdu, explore the various aspects of love and the beloved is an almost constant presence in one way or the other. More often than not, it is either her beauty which is the subject of discourse or her faithlessness. The chief theme of a lot of poems by Faiz Ahmed Faiz too, is love. But often, simultaneously, Faiz delves deep into questions that are social, political and economic: questions which become as fundamental to existence, in moments of crises, as water is to life. He vehemently opposes injustice and inequality. The public events, the crises of the times in which he lived, affected his growth and development as a poet to such an extent that the pressures and the travails still pulsate in the poetry of this gifted writer. However, this is nothing new to Urdu poetry. Amongst others, Allama lqbal, the compatriot of Faiz Ahmed Faiz too was affected, to such an extent, by the events of the era in which he lived, that he wrote the famous poem 'Shikwa' and then the 'Jawab-ay-Shikwa'. Faiz was drawn to Marxism and by that route, to literature that was realistic. He himself says:

> During this period, my colleagues in college, two people who had come back from Oxford had become Marxists, and they introduced me to Marxism. Later on, a whole bunch of young men returned from British universities all belonging to rich or aristocratic families and all communists. Some of them stayed communist, others after dabbling in it for a few years, took on various jobs. Anyway, they came back and they started a literary movement which was called the Progressive

> Writers' Movement. It was not a Communist or a Marxist movement as such, at though many of the office holders belonged to this group, but it was a sort of realistic movement. Because previously during the classical period and the period afterwards, our poetry and our literature was very largely given up to legends and fanciful tales and romanticizing and poetry of very largely linguistic gymnastics. During this period, a genuine lyrical political poetry was born.
>
> At the same time during the 1930s, the great anti-fascist movement rose and the literary movements both in Europe and in America turned to literature of social comment. We got directly influenced by the movement and that is how between 1932 and 1955, I got involved in this political-cum-literary movement. Secondly, in trade unions and workers, peasants movements and thirdly, by creating a new style that was an amalgam both of lyricism and of politics, of classicism and modernism and that appealed to the people.

Faiz emerges as a poet of protest under the Socialist / Marxist movement of the 1930s. This ideology, in his case, is however not just skin deep but is germane to his thought process, conscious as he was of the plight of his countrymen under the British Raj in general and his co-religionists in particular, who laboured under the double burden of the colonised as well as that of illiteracy, poverty and squalor. Faiz declared:

> . . . as a writer, even though I run no state and command no power, I am entitled to feel that I am my brother's keeper and my brother is the whole of mankind . . But out of this vast brotherhood the nearest and dearest to me are the insulted, the humiliated, the homeless, the disinherited, the poor, the hungry and sick at heart. And this is the relevance to me of Palestine, of South Africa, Zimbabwe, of Chile, of my own people and people like me.

Faiz believed in brotherhood and humanism. His realistic approach to life and its problems is revealed by his poetry as well as his prose. His judgements are culled from human experience and rational thought as opposed to religious beliefs and convictions.

A number of poems by Faiz focus on or represent or resist the violence of colonisation, oppression, injustice and inequality. The poem entitled 'Hum Dekhenge' (We shall witness the day ordained) is one such poem. It is a poem of great hope for the have-nots of this world. Herein, Faiz dreams of a massive, all pervading revolution in which the downtrodden will turn the tables and there will be a complete reversal of roles. Tyrants will be violently decimated. This is inscribed on the "tablets of history" or the *lauh-e-azal.* History is witness to the fact that all tyrants are vanquished some day or the other. There is a perfect expression for this in Persian: *Har Firaun-ay raah Moosa (to each Pharaoh, there is a Moses).* Every tyrant shall be vanquished by an appropriate agent. Here Faiz foretells the destruction of tyrants at the hands of a marching multitude of the down-trodden.

> When massive mountains of cruelty and tyranny
> Will be blown sky-high like fluffs of cotton;
> When marching steps of the downtrodden
> Will make the earth beneath their feet quake and shudder
> When skies above the heads of tyrant rulers
> By streaks of lighting are split asunder
> We will see!

Set in the environs of Islamic ideology, the third and the fourth stanzas declare that false gods will be vanquished, their crowns and thrones, thought to be the symbols of absolute power, will be destroyed. The seats of power thus vacated, will be inherited by the have-nots and the unwanted by the grace of the Almighty. The name of Allah will prevail; it is he who is the final inheritor. The master-stroke comes when very deftly Faiz re-interprets the term *anal haq* or 'I am the truth' which is understood to be the prerogative of the Almighty alone, to include "you and I", that is common man. The expression: *anal haq* has, for long, been a bone of contention between the orthodox and the liberal and the dice has always been loaded heavily in favour of the orthodox. History bears testimony that a number of sufi saints have been persecuted and killed for repeatedly saying *anal haq* . Here Faiz uses it not only to symbolise freedom and equality but also raises the banner of revolt against orthodoxy. This is an acute form of protest. Also, Faiz seems to believe along with Frantz Fanon that:

> ... unless national consciousness at its moment of success was somehow changed into social consciousness, the future would not hold liberation but an extension of imperialism.

In this poem, the colonised subject or the suppressed classes spin out of the hegemonic control of the elite power groups and declare their independence.

The poem 'Dogs' is a protest against the indolence of the masses who lack a sense of dignity, since they do not react, in spite of the humiliation heaped on them. They lack motivation and purpose in life and make no effort to improve their condition. As a result they live like destitutes and beggary is their lot. They are surrounded by dirt and filth and the drain is their home. Though inaction is their forte most of the time, when they are aroused, they can be made to quarrel amongst themselves for petty gains. The coloniser or master is able to divert them with the help of insignificant material benefits and skillfully applies the policy of divide and rule. Faiz says that they are unaware of their own power and would be quite a force to reckon with, if they would but realise this. Urging them to action, Faiz declares that the day the masses are aroused, imperialism will come to a violent end. Faiz visualises a situation which would be similar to the Revolutions that took place in Europe during 1830 - 1848. Hence, this poem is a protest against the rule of a privileged minority over a suppressed majority and makes a call for action on the part of the suppressed masses. It is an effort on the part of Faiz to respond to the crisis of the period and in its call for "action" has a close parallel, in a poem written by W. H. Auden, during this period:

> So in this hour of crisis and dismay,
> What better than your strict and adult pen

Can warn us from the colours and the consolations,
The showy arid works, reveal
The squalid shadow of academy and garden,
Make action urgent and its nature clear?
Who give us nearer insight to resist
The expanding fear, the savaging disaster?6

The ability to speak is a unique human ability. But often, such is the state that all human beings may not have this opportunity to express themselves. Those who are of inferior rank or are subject to the hegemony of the dominant or the ruling classes are often denied even this fundamental right bestowed on man by nature. The title of a beautiful poem by Faiz is *Bol* which means 'Speak up'. Just as the poem 'Kutty' or 'Dogs' urges the masses to action, in the same way 'Bol' insists on self expression. Though your body is in chains, your lips are free, says Faiz. Written in the backdrop of imperialism and bondage, with forceful images like those of a "red oven", "fierce flames", "padlocks" and "fetters" the poem urges people to speak and thus define themselves. A sense of urgency is forcefully communicated by the lines:

Speak up, for your lips are not sealed
And your words are still your own.
This upright body is yours
Speak; while your soul is still your own.

Look there, in that smithy,
Its red oven, fierce flames,
The padlocks are already opening their mouths
And each fetter is skirting around.

Speak up now, for time's running out.
Before your body and mind fade away,
Tell us, for truth is not yet dead.

This poem is a protest against imperialism and bondage which includes the denial of voice to those who have been colonised or are of an inferior class, socially or inferior because they are powerless.

'Ask Me Not for That Old Fervour My Love' presents the poet as a divided house, one whom romance and reality, both beckon. This dilemma is central to a number of poems by Faiz such as 'Poesy's Domain'. This poem 'Ask Me Not for That Old Fervour My Love' is a direct address to his beloved and begins with the request that his beloved should not expect him to love her with an exclusive ardour, to the utter disregard of everything else. He accepts, however, that he had imagined that her very presence in his life would obliterate the miseries of the entire world for him. But this did not happen. The world of love, unrequited or fulfilled, does not exist in isolation, though it is essentially a private world, but is part and parcel of the public world and this public world intrudes upon the private world of an individual, the poet realises. Hence, he regretfully requests his beloved not to expect him to love her in the same romantic way that he had done earlier. His is a more realistic approach now, in spite of the fact that she is as beautiful and adorable as ever. The images of suffering that the poet presents in this poem, highlight a social consciousness that is characteristic of the writers of this period.

Samuel Hynes, while discussing the literature and politics in England during this period opines: It is not surprising that in the context of such events the imaginations of young people were becoming increasingly engaged with the issues of the public world. One can see this process taking place most clearly, by examining the undergraduate publications of Oxford and Cambridge. The Oxford Outlook, which had been Oxford's principal journal of arts and letters since the war, suddenly changed its nature with the issue of May 1932. Richard Goodman, a student-poet who was also a Marxist, became editor, and in his first issue featured Middleton Murry on 'Communism and the Universities' (in which Murry exhorted students to become communists), a short story about German workers, and his own poem, 'The Manifesto', full of red flags and marching masses. The journal then ceased publication, to appear a year later as the New Oxford Outlook, with a strong left-wing political leaning; 'the present editors believe,' an editorial explained, 'that there is now coming into existence, some attitude, some outlook, in fact less transient than the post-war poses.' In the first issue this new outlook was expressed in an editorial on the economic situation, an essay on 'How Nazis Think', and a poem entitled 'Diary of a Revolutionary'. And in the second by a piece on 'Fascism and Communism in Oxford'. The change from the 'post-war poses' is clear, and so is the students' self-conscious self-approval that they have made it.

At Cambridge a new journal, 'Cambridge Left,' began in the summer of 1933. There, too, the change in student consciousness is a subject for comment. In the first issue this 'Note on Poetry and Politics' appeared:

> The motives for writing of those who are writing for this paper, have changed, along with their motives for doing anything. It is not so much an intellectual choice, as the forcible intrusion of social issues.
>
> Those who are left in their politics have to face certain problems as writers of prose or verse. Most of the present contributors are' aware of the problems, but to formulate them successfully would be, to have solved them. So it is most profitable to try and solve them by trial and error. That is what is attempted in this paper.

The 'forcible intrusion of social issue' is very much like Spender's phrase about being hounded by external events: both are accounts of that harsh invasion of the private life by public crises that is so definitive a part of the experience of the 'thirties' generation.

Stephen Spender had also written "From 1931 onwards, in common with other people, I felt hounded by external events." Faiz has the same relevance and position in the context of national and international events, here in the Indian Sub-continent as that which is enjoyed by Auden and his generation of poets in England.

'The Morning of Freedom, August 1947' highlights the chasm that exists between the ideal and the real. Forceful imagery indicates that the moment of the fulfillment of a long cherished, hard earned dream is not the type of liberation that was sought and hoped for. Conspicuously absent is the exhilaration that should have accompanied the declaration of Independence. The focus is on the eruption of violence, the bloody communal clashes which accompanied Independence and the partition of the country. Hence, the Independence is "pock-marked" or full of blemishes. The poem throbs with agony and anguish. This is not the kind of independence that could be a cause of celebration for Faiz. This poem also effectively challenges the popular notion that liberation from foreign bondage would necessarily alter the fate of the weak, the downtrodden and the suppressed. Faiz believed, and rightly so, that the "major cultural problems of underdeveloped countries" are "related to the organisation, values and practices of a backward social structure" which "can be effectively solved only when the political revolution of national liberation is followed by a social revolution to complete national independence". Since this too is missing, there is a lack of deja vu on the part of the poet.

The execution of the Rosenberg couple in the United States of America in 1951, accused of spying for the Soviet Union - had a profound impact on Faiz Ahmed Faiz and he wrote a poignant poem entitled 'We who were slain in unlit pathways' full of a tragic consciousness, that comes through empathy. Not only did Faiz share the sympathy that the Rosenbergs had for the Soviet Union, a communist country but he was as a communist, also moved by the supreme sacrifice of the Rosenbergs, the unflinching loyalty to a cause that they believed in, a state which brings out the best in man; the best in this case led to the gallows and death. The Rosenbergs are perceived as die-hard communist activists by Faiz. He celebrates their bravery and staunch belief and was convinced that their martyrdom would inspire more legions to follow in their footsteps. The Rosenbergs proved their faithfulness to the cause they believed in, by facing the electric chair. The poem celebrates human determination and steadfastness. It is an epitome of communist ideology in poetic attire. The trial of the Rosenbergs is mired in controversy with Jean Paul Satre calling the trial "a legal lynching which smears with blood, a whole nation." The unlit pathways of the poem refer to this denial of justice to Julius and Ethel Rosenberg. The memory of this execution also reverberates in "The Bell Jar"- a novel by Sylvia Plath - which has been praised for its effective portrayal of the tensions of the era in question. Faiz is one with other literary writers of his era, in other far flung parts of the globe in taking up an issue which is an international one and whose rumblings have been heard as recently as 2008 with Morton

Sobell admitting that he, Julius Rosenberg and David Greenglass spied for the Soviet Union. It is poems like 'We who were executed in unlit pathways' and 'Battle Ground,' and another poem, wherein he portrays the violence in Beirut, the capital of Lebanon situated in the middle-east, that testify to the width of his canvas. In spite of his romantic leanings, Faiz emerges as a committed artist who responds to the world around him in a sensitive way and writes in an emotive manner, so that he becomes an inspiration for others who do not have his felicity with words, his analytic ability and clarity of outlook. A fierce lover of freedom, an independent thinker, he protests and revolts against injustice, inequality and tyranny. The protest, the revolutionary fervour of his poetry, is not only the hallmark of the major poets of that era, world over but also a response to a time which was somehow out of joint and the poetry of Faiz Ahmed Faiz not only says so but also provides the impetus and the zeal to set things right.

Purushottam Agrawal*

"It has been decreed again that you and I be exiled..."

Sajjad Zaheer had described the publication of 'Zindan Nama' as 'the most important historical event of the year 1952 in the history of Pakistan.' And, indeed, not only this collection, but other poetic works of Faiz, deserve to be celebrated not only as literary events, but also as historical events of larger significance. Not only because, Faiz the citizen directly engaged with politics, but also because, Faiz the poet, articulated the universal yearnings of human soul in a particular historical context with unique involvement. It is precisely because of the adroit handling of this dialectics that Faiz has transcended the boundaries of political space and historical time. He continues to fascinate the readers and listeners, particularly in the Indian sub-continent, and particularly the young of all ages. His personal life with its adventurous ups and downs and his status as a world-citizen adds to the fascination and aura around both his persona and poetry. I still have the vivid memories of the tumultuous welcome he received in JNU and at other places in the year 1980. In fact, the exhilaration, his mere presence caused and the sense of achievement, that Suman (my wife) could manage to get his autograph on our copy of Hindi version of 'Shishon ka Masiha' was one of the headiest memories in our life. To quip on a famous line from another great of Urdu poetry - Firaq Gorakhpuri - The future generations would be proud of us who have seen Faiz!

Faiz essentially is a poet of romance. The tension is his poetry - which makes it so poignant - emanates from the constant dialogue between the romance of erotic love and the romance of revolution. The poet, in the early phase seems to be positing an irreconcilable contradiction between

---

* Purushottam Agrawal is a Member of Union Public Service Commission (UPSC), New Delhi and a renowned Hindi critic.

longing of love and that of revolutionary change; it was in tune with the early phase of progressive writing:

> The world knows sorrows other than those of love
>
> Pleasures beyond those of romance

But even here, if you read the poem in its entirety, it is the pain of love and revolution not being possible simultaneously, that makes the poem what it is- an evergreen chant of nostalgic yearning for love. The poetic meaning of the poem clearly transcends the 'intended message'.

As times passed, the poetic self of Faiz transformed the apparent 'contradiction' between love and revolution into the dialogue between the two. This dialogue compliments and completes both the participants; makes everything other than the fundamental quest of the poet (and of the audience as well) redundant. Here the choices are rather sharply defined. The poetic self does not brook anything other than the finality of love and the end- death- itself.

> No place on the way seemed worth its while
>
> From the beloved's street, I headed straight to the gallows

Faiz's everlasting popularity is generally attributed to his powerful evocation of the democratic sensibility through poignant images and deft employment of poetic diction. Ironically, such popularity sometimes serves, in fact depends upon, reading him as a one-dimensional poet, which most certainly he is not. His political poems are effective, because as poems, these are not merely political. He consciously evokes the memories of the poets of past and also uses his cultural and religious legacy in a very creative and innovative way. The idea of other world, life after death, is common to all religious traditions, and is equally alien to the political ideology, consciously upheld by the poet. But he uses this idea to make a moral point in an enthralling way. The poem has the creative ambiguity, making it possible to grasp political commitment as well as commitment in love - suffering being the linking thread.

The tension between ideology and creativity is not prominent in his poetry. But he still appeals to even those who might not share his ideology, because, his commitment does not blind him to the really poignant moments of the every-day life. Neither does it take him away from the articulation of the real dilemmas of a poet. The search for the correct word and the suitable idiom is the most fundamental search for any serious poet. Faiz is not only aware of this, not only does he constantly work on this, but also 'says' it most exquisitely - the mere presence of him/her, changed what I wanted to say.

His poetry, taken as a whole, actually creates an ambience of hope and despair, utopia and nostalgia. He lived as a 'world-citizen' alright, but his heart bled for his own place. While in a reflective mood, in dialogue with his own self, he knew his fate, and lamented it:

> My heart, my fellow traveler
>
> It has been decreed again
>
> That you and I be exiled
>
> To go calling out in every street
>
> Turn to every town
>
> To search for a clue
>
> For a messenger from our beloved
>
> To ask every stranger
>
> The way back to our home

Is not such an exile, the fate of many, who choose to impart some meaning to existence? Is it not true of even humbler human beings that they also are sometimes forced to ask every stranger "the way back to home"?

Sohail Hashmi*

Faiz - The Poet of Romance and Revolution

If you met him on the street you would never imagine that he was a poet, and not your run of the mill poet, but among the most important poets of the 20th century, not only in Urdu, not only in the subcontinent but in the entire world of the 20th century. I have always wondered how could someone who invariably dressed in rather unimpressively stitched, unromantic Terri-Cot Safari suits, someone who could, at best, pass off as a joint secretary in the ministry of shipping or something similar, be such a wizard with words and not only with words but with content and with form?

The answer to this question lies perhaps in the linguistic, cultural traditions that Faiz had inherited, the extent to which Faiz was able to build upon, deepen and add to this inheritance through his own reading and through the insightful guidance of his teachers like Maulvi Mohammad Sialkoti, Shams-ul-Ulema Syed Mir Hasan, Professor Yusuf Salim Chishti, Ahmed Shah 'Pitras' Bukhari, Sufi Ghulam Mustafa 'Tabassum', Maulvi Mohammad Shafi, Dr Mohammad Deen Taseer, Maulana Abdul Majid Salik, Maulana Chiragh Hasan 'Hasrat' and Pandit Hari Chand 'Akhtar'.

In fact, the tradition goes back into the past, a few centuries if not more and it may not be a bad idea to trace the tradition, upon which Faiz meticulously built the grand, imposing and, dare I, say everlasting edifice of his poetic discourse.

Over the last three centuries, Urdu has produced one great poet every 100 years or so, the 18th Century was the century of Meer, the 19th

---

* Sohail Hashmi is a cultural activist and writer. He is a founding trustee of Safdar Hashmi Memorial Trust (SAHMAT), New Delhi.

belonged to Ghalib and the 20th was the century of Faiz. Whether this trend will continue in the present century, though, seems a little doubtful.

There have naturally been many other significant poets in these three hundred years but and this is a big but, there have not been too many aside from these three that have created a new discourse in poetics.

Meer was to use the metaphor of the broken, shattered, distraught heart to describe both his own personal loss as also the pillage and destruction of Delhi, an adopted city that he came to love and hold dear, not only physically but also metaphorically. The deserted streets and empty houses became symbols of the passing away of a lifestyle and an aesthetic urbane milieu.

Ghalib was to infuse the Ghazal with a depth and a multi-layerity that the form had not hitherto seen. Ghalib also contributed significantly to freeing the *Ghazal* from the constricting grip of a cold heartless beloved, a successful rival and the perpetually unsuccessful lover - the poet - drowning himself in wine or wallowing in masochistic self pity.

There were others before him, Wali 'Daccani' and Meer Taqi Meer to name just two, who too contributed to this broadening of the horizons of the Ghazal. What Ghalib did was to introduce content that had, by and large, not been explored by versifiers. Ghalib raised fundamental questions of existence and being, raised doubts about received world views and established that the *Ghazal* was capable of tackling complex ideas. The imagery of Ghalib's poetry, drew as much from his immediate surroundings as it did from the rich heritage of Central Asia that had in turn drawn from the myths of ancient Greece and Egypt, tales and fables that also resonated in the Torah, the Bible and the Quraan.

Ghalib lived in strange times, an order was dying and the new was yet to replace it, Ghalib was a witness to these cataclysmic times. The rapid collapse of the Mughal court led to the replacement of a system of patronage with unending uncertainty and penury. The revolt took away with it, the last vestiges of an order that India had known and the ruthless crushing of the uprising, led to an era of unprecedented changes, whose impact was to inform the creation of literature in a fundamental and far reaching manner.

The rhythm and organisation of life, its ethos and aesthetics, the system of patronage, everything that gave a sense of continuity to life - of the period was changing, mutating and getting transformed. Ghalib, like many of his contemporaries, was deeply shaken by these events and suffered the consequences of this upheaval.

It is in times such as these that questions began to be raised about the capacity of the *Ghazal* to encapsulate these rapid changes and to express them in a tangible and intelligible manner. Ghalib was among those who tried to address this question and was to say:

> The range of the *Ghazal* is inadequate - I need a larger canvas for my expression[1]

Questions began to be raised about received ideas and accepted world views, new forms of expression began to be explored, prose made its mark, Urdu Journalism began to come into its own and both verse and prose began to engage with this ever changing world. In terms of creativity this was among the most fertile periods for Urdu and for many other Indian languages.

The *Ghazal*, even as it was being challenged, began to explore newer areas of expression and non-Ghazal verse like the *Marsia* (the elegy) the *Masnavi* (long narrative poems) had begun to make their mark. This is also the time when poets began to move out of the traditional themes of poetry writing and poetry as political commentary became increasingly acceptable; this trend received a big fillip with the publication of the 'Musaddas' by Khwaja Altaf Husain 'Hali'.

The process of social comment in poetry had gradually been gathering steam for a while, Jafar Zattali's street-wise satire about corrupt and debauch nobility in the miniscule reign of Farrukhsiar (1713-1719) and Nazeer Akbarabadi's (1735-1830) long poems about poverty, hunger, old age, old prostitutes and eunuchs and about all kinds of artisans, street performers

---

[1]BaqDr-e-Shauq nahin, zarf-e-tangna-e-Ghazal
Kuchh aur chaahiye wus'at mere bayaN ke liye --- GHALIB.

and the like had begun to lay the ground for a new poetic and literary discourse. Jafar had to pay with his life for heaping scorn on Farrukhsiar. He was executed on the orders of the king in 1713 and Nazeer was virtually ignored till the late nineteenth century and had to wait till the 1950s, to get his due.

The devastation that was visited upon Delhi, Lucknow and vast areas of India in the aftermath of 1857, led, on the one hand to a sense of hopelessness and constant harking back to a glorious past and, on the other hand, to a seething anger against the British and their collaborators. The former was to trigger several reformist movements while the latter fed the growing anti-imperialist mood, leading to mass mobilizations and also to the creation of the poetry and prose of protest.

Both the reformists and the anti-imperialists used the written word, prose and verse to communicate their ideas and despite a handful of, largely ignored dissenters, the debate between art for art's sake versus art for life's sake was settled in favour of the latter, rather quickly.

Ghalib died in extreme penury in 1869, while Faiz published his first collection in 1941. Many new trends in poetics, that had begun to emerge in the time of Ghalib, had developed rapidly during the intervening 70 years.

The rapid decay of the Mughal empire and its vestiges, the replacement of the traditional patterns of patronage, the large scale collapse of traditional crafts, the increasing destitution of large sections of population was leading to a glorification of the past, and at another to a search for alternatives to these devastating changes and to calls for Indians to take their fate into their own hands and recapture the past glory of India. Echoes of these sentiments were to be heard in Hali and later in Iqbal. So the question that Ghalib had raised, with reference to need of a larger canvas, was answered through the emergence of the *Nazm*, in the main, through the writing of Iqbal.

Iqbal's contribution to the evolution of the *Nazm* is substantial and if there is one poet who can claim a place among the greats along with Meer, Ghalib and Faiz it can only be Iqbal. It is perhaps his engagement with the ideas of *Khudi* (being, self, ego) and Pan-Islamism ideas that did not have too many takers among the intellectuals of the 20th century and therefore despite impressing a large number of those that appreciated him, Iqbal failed to leave behind, a continuing poetic tradition.

In spite of the fact that his ideas did not have a large following, the vehicle, i.e. the *Nazm*, that he chose, to carry his ideas among the Urdu reading public, left a lasting impact and the *Nazm* was, in the early decades of the 20th century, put to effective use by a very large number of poets, who were writing against colonial depredation and using the *Nazm* to mobilize public opinion.

Despite these developments, the *Ghazal* did not yield ground easily; in fact for a while the upholders of 'tradition' strongly resisted this new onslaught, initially of metred and later of the unmetred *Nazm*. The *Nazm* did not replace the *Ghazal* fully; in fact till much later there were not too many poets who took to this new form to the total exclusion of the *Ghazal.* Even Iqbal, who can rightly claim credit for firmly establishing the *Nazm*, continues to use the *Ghazal* for political comment, for instance:

> Race, Nationalism, Church (religion) and colour
>
> How cleverly have the masters invented excuses[2]

The time that Faiz appears on the poetic scene with his first slim collection of poetry in 1941, is the time when the entire subcontinent is in ferment. Faiz is already recognized as a powerful new voice, he has met Dr. Rashid Jahan, Mohammad Deen Taseer, Syed Sajjad Zaheer and in 1936, becomes one of the founders of the All India Progressive Writers' Association (AIPWA) or PWA as it popularly came to be known.

The time when Faiz became secretary of the PWA in Punjab he was only 25. Mohammad Deen Taseer was 39, and both Sajjad Zaheer and Rashid Jahan were 37. Obviously, this young man had built a reputation even at this young age, for compared to him these three were seasoned campaigners.

---

[2]Nasl, Qaumiyat, Kaleesa, Sultanat Tehzeeb Rang
Khwwajgi ne khoob chun chun kar banaaye maskraat ---- Iqbal

Rashid Jahan and Sajjad Zaheer along with Ahmed Ali and Mahmud-uz-Zafar had contributed to *Angaarey (Embers)*-a collection of short stories that had triggered a storm among the conservatives, because the stories attacked the oppression of women in the name of religion, they attacked superstition and feudalism. Angaarey was banned in 1933 by the colonial government, because the book "hurt the religious sentiments of a particular community".

It was the banning of the book that eventually led to the formation of the PWA, an organisation committed to oppose imperialism, fascism, feudalism and to work, for the spread of progressive ideas through literature and to fight for an end to exploitation of man by man. Incidentally Mohammad Deen Taseer married a British leftist Christabel and Faiz was to later marry Alys, the younger sister of Christabel. The recently assassinated Governor of Punjab, in Pakistan, was the son of Mohammad Deen Taseer and Christabel and a nephew of Alys and Faiz.

The PWA held its first conference in Lucknow, presided over by Munshi Prem Chand in 1936 and Faiz became the secretary of PWA, Punjab in the same year.

The PWA and Faiz with it, represented a continuation of a tradition that was rooted in the people-centric poetry of Nazeer, a tradition that, like Meer, saw personal tragedies and sufferings as part of a larger social loss, a tradition that had, from the time of Ghalib, begun to move away consciously from hackneyed themes in poetry and imbue poetry with meaning, engaging itself with complex thoughts and ideas to question and reject the ossified moribund and inane discourse of 'conversations with the beloved' that the *Ghazal* had been reduced to, a tradition that had roots in the reformist zeal of Hali and his contemporaries and most significantly a tradition that was inspired by the struggle against imperialism and oppression going back to the 1857 revolt of the peasants and the Sepoys. The poetic and literary tradition that Faiz and his comrades upheld was also a tradition that had as its precursors, the literary campaigners for change, like Iqbal.

Faiz, like many of his contemporaries, had the advantage of drawing from the traditional cultural resources and scholarship of the Persian and

Arabic literature. Faiz incidentally had done his masters in both Arabic and English Literature. He had begun to study Arabic, Persian and Urdu from early childhood.

Faiz's father, Sultan Mohammad Khan had begun life as a shepherd who was paid to look after the animals of the village for two rupees, a month. The young shepherd had a thirst for knowledge and education that saw him overcoming almost impossible odds, to rise to the position of the chief secretary of Abdul Rehman Khan, the then king of Afghanistan, being appointed the Ambassador of Afghanistan in Britain, studying Law in London, becoming a barrister and returning to Sialkot, to practice and being decorated with the title of Khan Bahadur. When Khan Bahadur, Sultan Mohammad Khan died, he was under a colossal debt and his children had to sell off most of his property, to pay off the debts.

So Faiz had seen it all, growing up in plenty, losing it all in his early youth and then having to rebuild his life, virtually from scratch. Along the way he taught, edited literary Journals, served as war correspondent, edited *Pakistan Times* and *Imroz*, worked actively in Trade Unions, was arrested on charges of Conspiracy, spent years in jail, more years in exile, was awarded the Lenin Peace Prize, edited *Lotus* from Beirut, even when the city was bombed and throughout this tumultuous life, he continued to write - 7 volumes of poetry, and almost as many in prose, including critical essays, memoirs, articles on a diverse range of issues and much more.

In the short speech that Faiz made, while accepting the Lenin Peace Prize, Faiz said, "I do not find anything in my writing or my conduct that qualifies me for this great Award, the only reason that I can think of is the fact that the great ideals that I and my friends have been associated with, that is the desire for peace and freedom, are ideals that are so grand and beautiful that even those associated with them, even though peripherally, acquire respectability[3]." He concluded the speech with these words:

> I am confident that humanity that has never accepted defeat at the hands of its enemies will once again emerge victorious and finally the

---

[3]Reproduced in Dast Tah-e-Sang pp. 9-12

> foundations of our mutual existence will be laid not on war, hate, oppression and acrimony but something that had been pointed out by the Persian poet Hafiz a long time ago:
>
> Faulted are the foundations of all that I have seen
> But for the foundation of Love that alone is faultless[4]

His remarks about his being undeserving of the Lenin Peace Prize and his confidence in the ultimate victory of the human spirit are things that define Faiz, he was humble and this humility was not an act, it was not put on, all those who were with him in jail for four years and more, have in their writings and recollections talked about his gentle and undemanding nature. He was gentle, humble and steadfast in his commitment; his poetry drew strength from these two constituents of his being. Joan Baez, one of the most popular singers of the Anti-Vietnam War campaign in the US, used to sing a song that was titled "And what have they done to the rain" and before she sang the song she once said, 'this is a very powerful song, because it protests gently'. What she was probably suggesting, was that if you stand with just causes, with truth, you do not have to shout from roof tops, your conviction in justice and truthfulness shines through even without unnecessary aggression. Faiz was like that and so was his poetry.

Faiz was soft spoken, genial, affable, and polite to a fault, spoke little, and rarely got into arguments, what he had to say, he said through his pen, more powerfully in verse and more like a tolerant teacher, in his prose. The sole source of the adulation that he received and also the brickbats, the persecution, the imprisonment, was his writing. Left to himself, he would not hurt a fly, he was probably afraid of lizards. That is the idea one gets from recollections of those who were with him in prison and yet his poetry talks of revolution, of snatching crowns, toppling thrones, of uncontrollable rivers in spate. His poem, 'Beware of My Being' on Bangladesh, speaks in the voice of the oppressed, warning all oppressors to steer clear, ' beware, for I am an ocean of Venom'.[5]

---

[4]Khalal Pezeer Buwad Har Bina ke mi beeni Bajuz benaaye mohabbat ke khaali az khalal ast

[5]Hazar Karo Mere Tan se ye Sam ka Darya hai Sar-e-Wadi-e-Sienna pp. 85-86

Where did such a soft spoken man, such a harmless looking soul, draw the strength for verses such as these? In the stray interviews and conversations that Faiz had, with his friends and his prison mates, he fondly remembers all his teachers and almost all of his collections begin with a couplet from one of the masters like Ghalib, Saadi, Sauda, Meer, Iqbal, Hafiz and Bedil; he underlines his debt to his literary inheritance.

Many of his teachers, that he was close to, were drawn towards the progressive movement, the impact of the Socialist revolution in Russia had stirred up the colonised people all over the world. The rise of Fascism was seen as a threat to all freedom loving people and the formation of the PWA must have come as a catalytic force that gave a purpose and direction to Faiz's writing.

The solid grounding in the classical languages, the opportunity to be a favourite pupil of some of the finest minds in Lahore of the 30s, his exposure to, and deep interest in, English and Western literature, generally and progressive literature particularly, provided him a larger canvas. He, more than many of his contemporaries, was able to draw profitably from these diverse resources and the result was visible from his early writings.

Languages, cultures, the arts - painting, music, poetry and prose- flourish in times of flux, in times of great upheavals and turmoil, for it is in times such as these that cross pollination of ideas, of content and form takes place at an unprecedented scale. The formative years of Faiz, the years when he was growing up, were times of great flux. There was the ever growing upsurge of popular resistance to colonial oppression, when Jalianwallah Bagh Massacre took place, Faiz was barely 8, but when Bhagat Singh was hanged Faiz was 20.

These were epochal times and Faiz was drawn to the ideals of Freedom, Equality and Socialism. Faiz was attracted to these ideas like so many others including Raghupati Sahay 'Firaq' Gorakhpuri, Shabbir Hasan Khan, 'Josh' Malihabadi, Asrar ul Haq 'Majaz', Moin Ahsan 'Jazbi', Jan Nisar 'Akhtar', Ali Sardar Jafri, 'Majrooh' Sultanpuri, 'Kaifi' Azmi and others, who were drawn to and influenced by these events and developments.

So aside from his inheritance and his own addition to this inheritance and what he imbibed from his teachers, the two other elements, that had a defining influence on Faiz and his poetry were, firstly the all encompassing sentiment for freedom, no one could escape the subterranean simmering that threatened to explode any moment, and did from time to time, and, secondly, the growing influence of Marxism and the fight against Fascism that intellectuals, poets, writers, artists, film makers and others were joining in large numbers all over the world. Behind this upsurge, was, of course the ideal of building an equitable and just order and to stand with the soviet people, who formed the vanguard against Fascism.

All these elements combined in the writing of Faiz to give it a unique colour. His vocabulary, his symbols, his similes were rooted deeply in the traditional diction of Urdu; even when he coined new expressions, he drew from the large traditional reservoir that he had at his disposal and the cadence did not sound alien to the listener.

Writing about the poetry of Majaz, Faiz had once said: 'what distinguishes Majaz from other progressive writers is the fact that he sings of the beauty of the revolution... he is not a drummer boy for the revolution'. This comment aptly describes almost all of Faiz's poetry as well.

While talking about his own understanding of the place of literature and the role of the writer he was to say:

> To be aware of the collective struggle of Humanity and to participate in this struggle to the best of one's ability, is a demand that life places upon us, literature too places the same demand upon us...... Art is a constituent of this life and the creative struggle is one aspect of this (wider) struggle."[6]

What is unique in the writing of Faiz is his grasp of both the *Ghazal* and the *Nazm*. Faiz was equally dexterous in both forms, many of his contemporaries tried their hand at both forms but some were known as

---

[6]Faiz, preface to Dast-e-Saba, pp. 5-6, written in Central Jail Hyderabad 16.9.1952

poets of the Ghazal and others were poets of the *Nazm*, but Faiz is equally at ease, in both forms.

Faiz was one of the accused in the so called Rawalpindi Conspiracy case. Faiz, Major Mohammad Is'haaq, and some other accused were kept in the Montgomery Central Jail, Sajjad Zaheer was sent to the Central Jail, Machh in Baluchistan while Captain Poshni and Ata Mohammad were despatched to the Central Jail, Hyderabad. Major Is'haaq used to mail Faiz's latest writings to the other accused in different jails. Sajjad Zaheer wrote to Major Is'haaq about 'Unrequited Love', a *ghazal* of Faiz that he had received a few days earlier. The letter has been reproduced by Major Is'haaq in 'The Prison Chronicle'.[7]

> "This ghazal that you call Wasokht is a fine work, each Sher is like a scaple, each one deserves praise and appreciation especially
>
> > If we worried about our wounds, we were accused
> > Of not singing paeans to the artistry of the sword wielder [8]
>
> Say nothing of Ja'afar Ali Khan 'Asar', Faiz would have received appreciation for this, even from Mirza Nausha (Ghalib)."

Jafar Ali Khan 'Asar' Lakhnawi, one of the finest critics of Urdu literature, especially of progressive Urdu literature was to assess Faiz in the following words:

> The poetry of Faiz, having risen through various stages of development has scaled heights that have perhaps never been reached by any other progressive writer.

Ghalib had complained of the limited canvas of the *Ghazal,* to Faiz must go the credit of expanding the horizons of the *Ghazal* and for firmly establishing the political *Ghazal* as a form distinct from the *Gul-o-Bulbul,*

---

[7]Roodaad-e-Qafas, Zindaan Naamaah pp 9-46

[8]Gar fikr-e-zakhm ki to khataawaar hain kr hum - Kyon mahv-e- madh-e-khoobi-e- tegh-e-ada na thay.

Hijr-o-Visaal, Masjid-o-Maikhana-kind of dichotomies that the Ghazal had come to be known for. Unfortunately among many well meaning fans of the form, it continues to be known as such, thanks to singers and listeners who refuse to explore changes in the form and the content of the *Ghazal* and continue to wallow in empty sentimental prattle. To Faiz must also go the credit, for establishing that meanings and possibilities that lay concealed within the recesses of the layered raiment of the *Ghazal*, presented possibilities that poetry and poets had still to explore.

Faiz and Majrooh, among others, contributed significantly to the evolution of the Political *Ghazal*. There has been a suggestion that Majrooh initiated the process before Faiz, but the fact remains that the Political *Ghazal* as we know it today, owes much more to its popularity through Faiz than it does through the writings of Majrooh.

Majrooh, decidedly one of the leading lights of the PWA, did not get the kind of recognition he deserved, perhaps due to a much smaller body of work, also because unlike Faiz he did not remain in the thick of political turmoil and so his poetry was not as sought after as was Faiz's. The rather abrupt and at times abrasive manner of Majrooh could have also contributed to this. These things should not, ideally, count in an objective assessment of a writer's worth, but unfortunately they do. Despite what others might say, Majrooh himself recognized the contribution of Faiz to progressive poetry in the subcontinent and said "Faiz was the Meer Taqi Meer of the Progressives." This is high praise indeed. Ghalib who was loath to acknowledge anyone as his superior recognized only Bedil and Meer as Ustads (great teachers) so when Majrooh describes Faiz as the Meer of the progressives, he is giving him an exalted position. One needs to remember that Majrooh can never be accused of excess, not in the area of appreciating others, at least.

What sets Faiz above his contemporaries in both the Nazm and the *Ghazal* is his rich vocabulary, his ability to draw upon mythological symbols, events, references and fables and to reinterpret them[9], to create visual images

---

[9] Nisar Main Teri Galiyon ke....pp. 65-67 Dast-e-Saba and Hum dekhenge, Mere Dil Mere Musafir, pp. 53-54

in the mind of the reader, through a careful selection of words[10], and create new images through the use of Eisenstein like montages of clashing images[11].

The contribution of Faiz, except for a handful of post modernist detractors, who tried to belittle him, out of pique, unconcealed envy and perhaps a feeling of inadequacy, in the face of his talent, was recognized by most of his contemporaries and many of his seniors. Raghupati Sahay 'Firaq' Gorakhpuri, a senior in age by as much as 15 years, an extremely proud man and rather economical in his recognition of the talent of others, was to lavish fulsome praise on Faiz when he said:

> Faiz established a new school of Poetry, the creative skill, affection, creative dexterity and breadth of vision with which Faiz relates the event of love with other significant social concerns was something entirely new and worthwhile in the love poetry of Urdu.

Noon Meem Rashid, a contemporary poet and someone who was in the vanguard of those, who were at the time, experimenting with non rhyming or what was then called blank verse, spoke of Faiz in terms that are no less than laudatory:

> Faiz is alone among contemporary poets who, with his imagination, wishes to create an alluring heaven of pure beauty, but has also glimpsed the reality that lurks behind the golden drapes of beauty and romance.

Professor Aal-e-Ahmed Suroor, and Asar Lucknawi were two of the most respected critics of Urdu literature in their times and are read, consulted and quoted extensively in literary debates even to this day.

Suroor, in his earliest writings about Faiz, was to say: "The poetry of Faiz is like a resplendent rainbow consisting of pleasant influences of English Literature and worthwhile and valuable elements of the Asian civilization."

---

[10] Sarod-e-Shabana, Naqsh-e-Faryadi, p.15. Sham, Dast-e-Tah-e-Sang, p. 33, Manzar, Dast-e-Tah-e-Sang' p. 79,

[11] Pass Raho, Dast-e-tah-e-Sang, p. 73.

Syed Sajjad Zaheer, a contributor to *Angarey*, one of the moving spirits behind the formation of PWA, along with Mulk Raj Anand, Mahmood-uz-Zafar, a key accused in the Rawalpindi Conspiracy Case and a close associate of Faiz, was asked to write the preface of 'Zindan Nama' and this is what he had to say about Faiz's poetry:

> The values that the poetry of Faiz represents and upholds are the values of progressive humanity the world over, they are such an inseparable part of his writing that nowhere do they appear either to be different from our finest cultural and civilisational values, nor do they lead to any cleavage between the unique style of the poet and his soft, sweet and lyrical writing. His moving similes and metaphors carry the fragrance of our land, his ideas glisten with the truth and democratic ideals that enlighten the hearts of the overwhelming majority of our people. If the purpose of cultural development and growth is to free humans from material and spiritual poverty, fill their hearts with compassion, give them the strength of character and the vision to stand up for justice and truth and to, enrich our collective and individual lives both externally and internally, then the poetry of Faiz seeks to reach out and touch all these cultural goals.

Faiz was, in his own life time, translated in dozens of languages of the subcontinent and scores of other languages across the world. Alexander Surkov, a well known Urdu scholar from the erstwhile USSR, wrote the preface to the Russian translation of Faiz's poetry, the article was translated by Seher Ansaari[12] in Urdu. An English translation by the author, of the present piece is reproduced here to conclude this hurriedly put together piece. Translating poetry is not my cup of tea, what I have sought to do is to place a literal translation. The best way to appreciate Meer, Ghalib, Faiz and Iqbal is to learn their language:

---

[12] Ek Hausla Mand Dil ki Aawaaz, Sar-e-Vaadi-e-Sienna, pp.13-18

While we sat in a room in the office of the writers association in Moscow, reading poetry and talking about the possibility of publishing a Russian translation of Faiz's poetry, the conversation moved away from poetry to a discussion about contemporary politics:

'What are your plans in the immediate future ?'

Faiz looked at me, in the depths of his dark eyes I noticed a certain sadness while a gentle smile played on his lips, "I'll first go to London to meet a few friends who have recently arrived from Pakistan and then I'll go to Karachi, to Lahore, home....."

"But you know what it is like there....."

"All the more reason for me to go back to my country."

"Imprisonment then is a certainty........"

"Perhaps....... if serving a lofty ideal involves a trip to the jail, one must undertake the journey."

"And if it is worse than a prison term?"

The poet looked out of the window, at the Statute of Tolstoy in the middle of the garden, at the cold autumn sky, the smile was still there, a short pause later, he spoke, in his typical low and measured tone, "If there is something worse than a prison term, it will certainly be bad, but you know well the struggle has to carry on."

Suneet Chopra*

The Intellectual and National Integration

I met Faiz Ahmed Faiz in 1980, when he came to India for the *Jashn-e-Faiz.* He was a close friend of my mother's maternal uncle, Yugal Mehra of AIR (later Salman Ahmed of Pakistan Radio), the father of General Mehra, of the Indian Army and grandfather of Salma Agha, the Pakistani singer (the romance of whose grandparents is mentioned in Manto's 'My Bombay Friends'). When Faiz heard that he was my *nana* (grandfather), he said, "I am your *nana*, too" and gave me this interview:

Suneet Chopra: One of the main problems which the freedom movement in newly independent countries faced was that of uniting the different nationalities and national minorities of a colonial state, in the freedom struggle. How far was the leadership of the national movement of this subcontinent, able to overcome this problem?

Faiz Ahmed Faiz: To understand a multilingual and multinational state, we must first understand how such states come into being. Lenin has written in one of his articles, that a multinational state is the product of uneven development. This unevenness can be caused by many things. Foreign aggression can cause this, or one or more stronger nationalities, within the society can use their political power for subjugating the other small, weaker and less developed nationalities and can obstruct their further development. In this subcontinent, the problem arose because this country was colonised by the most powerful, widespread and brutal colonial power in the world: Britain. It was on the basis of their administrative necessities that the pre-existing linguistic and cultural boundaries were ignored, which in turn fostered a fertile ground for mutual hatred and riots. The vested interests

---

* Suneet Chopra is a Member of Central Committee of Communist Party of India (Marxist) - CPI (M). He is an eminent art critic.

of various stronger groups continued to strengthen these clashes and this hatred in the class societies, that came into being after the British left.

There are two main ways of dealing with the problem. First, while recognizing the separate language, culture and national development of each national, linguistic or ethnic group, to look for what they have in common among them. This can be called the approach of political and cultural pluralism. The protagonists of the other approach, that of strong centralisation, criticise this on the ground that, separatist tendencies are fanned by it. Their main weakness is that they regard cultural, linguistic and national diversity, as animosity. It is wrong to treat such differences as antagonistic.

It is obvious that the decision as to which of these two policies should be followed, is dependent on socio-economic structure of the countries comprising our subcontinent. In class society, the vested interests naturally accentuate differences of culture and language, attempt to dominate not only their own group, but also others.

The claim to a national identity also has two sides to it. When it is made with the interest of the masses in view, it becomes a progressive slogan. But when it is invoked in the interest of a handful of vested interests, its character can be reactionary. National integration too, is only possible when we openly and vocally stress the equal political, economic and social rights of all nationalities, constituting a multi-national state and when we are prepared to underline common problems, that plague the whole people like poverty and so on.

The writer's role is not confined to the analysis of their common interests, but must take into account their historical experience, social values and their day to day lives as well. Through his powers of perception, the writer must give it a creative and theoretical form as well. The writings should combat the chauvinism and separatism bred by vested interests and should strengthen the interaction between the experience and expression of different peoples.

Take the Progressive Writers' Association in India, for example. It reflected these ideas in a sound way. Then why did it come apart after

Independence? Before Independence, the struggle for freedom and anti-imperialism kept it together. But after Independence no such common basis, could be found. That is why this movement collapsed. I am not taking up the cause of a writers' association, owing allegiance to a particular political party, for writers would never accept such a limitation. I am referring to the necessity of an organisation, with a broad basis, but keeping in mind the new socio-economic and cultural conditions that emerged after Independence. The failure of the Progressive Writers' Association to evolve such a new social and political outlook, resulted in its break-up.

SC: What is your opinion regarding the conscious attempts of imperialism to sow dissensions among the masses?

FAF: The conspiracies of imperialism came out in the open during the transfer of power, most blatantly. The British Rulers had evolved many methods so that different nationalities and classes would fight among themselves, for crumbs from the imperialist table. What were their methods? Take representation in the Assemblies. They used not only a communal basis, but also favoured landlords, the Rajas and Nawabs, as well as narrow stratum of taxpayers for privileged representation. Then there was the question of reservation in the services not for backward classes, but on a communal basis. Education too, was divided on communal lines. Their language policy served those vested interests, who in the name of popular demands, fulfil their narrow class interest. This naturally affected our development seriously. Exclusive Hindu and Muslim prototypes were put forward so that the interaction that took place in the field of culture and of its colonial counter part ??. That was the aim of the British, in misrepresenting the composite culture of the subcontinent.

Urdu and Hindi are not different. The word Hindi itself is Persian. In reality, only the script is different, but the idiom is similar. Prem Chand could write in both Hindi and Urdu. The language of films too, underlines the common idiom of Hindi and Urdu. While it is true that the content of such films is poor, efforts should be made to improve it.

It is a great pity that the leaders of the national movement, like Gandhi did not pay as much attention to these aspects as they should have. And when they did, it was already too late.

SC: What did the leaders of the national movement do to deal with this problem?

FAF: They also used the same police and law and order machinery that the British had left behind. Along with this structure, they kept the social and economic exploitation, and oppression it buttressed, intact. What came into being economically, was a feudal and capitalist alliance, and not a democratic society. It was a society that preserved the evils of both feudalism and capitalism, without their good points. The national movement leaders accepted the old structure and did not bother to transform it in a progressive direction.

SC: According to you, what is the role of writers and intellectuals in furthering national integration? How far do you think their efforts meet the needs of the nationalities and national minorities of our subcontinent?

FAF: A writer can only present that reality which he perceives. His writing reflects all the complications and contradictions of his life. But he is not necessarily an agent of the State or part of its machinery, so he can make an effort to change the consciousness of his readers. In one way, he fulfills the same role in our society that the *sufis, bhakts* and humanist thinkers have done all along. While it is true that his basic contribution is his writing, he can only be effective when he takes part in the day-to-day experience of the people, that is, to share their politics also. This does not mean he should become a full-time politician, but it is necessary to share the political life of the people and to get intellectually and personally involved with the people, but this should not be taken too literally either. For example, it is not necessary for me to have gone to Vietnam to write about it, my knowledge can be a sufficient basis to identify myself with the struggle there.

SC: Have you worked among different nationalities and what was your experience among them?

FAF: Among trade unionists, the question of nationalities is not so important. But after partition this question came to the fore among writers and students. In 1960, I was a member of the first commission, set up to study the problem of national languages. We prepared a report, which took the view point that all the national cultures had an equal right to develop and that their development was no threat to national integration. In the late sixties, I was chairman of the Commission, which was expanded and made more democratic. We went into the problem deeply, interviewed 500 people, and consulted almost 300 cultural organisations spreading from Peshawar to Chittagong. On this basis we wrote out our recommendations, which were accepted by the Bhutto Government. In accordance with it, in 1972, a National Council of Art and Culture, came into being. We were able to use it to help the development of folk culture, to some extent. In our country, while a common classical tradition is observable, there is much more diversity at the level of folk culture but once you are able to establish a representative and development become obvious, there are many aspects of culture that do not reflect ethnic differences, but a geographical or other basis, as a result of which, the boundaries of ethnicity break down. I will never forget how Bade Ghulam Ali Khan used to demonstrate the common features of Pahari ragas, film songs, and even Alpine and Spanish mountain melodies. Today, we have a number of writers of different nationalities in Pakistan who have emerged, like the Sindhi poet Sheik Ayaz, the Baluchi Gul Khan Nasir, Pushto Ajmal Khattak, and Munir Niazi, a Punjabi.

SC: How did you as a writer, overcome the cultural and other social limitations of your birth?

FAF: Man must identify with something greater than himself. When I was a teacher in Amritsar I came in contact with the Trade Union Movement, where there were mainly textile workers, weavers by origin too. We used to go there at night and teach them. Afterwards, I left for Lahore. There I worked in the post and Telegraph Union and among Railway workers. Their president, Mirza Ibrahim was mostly in jail and I officiated for him as Vice President. I also represented the Pakistani working class at the world meet of the ILO. This was my first foreign trip. This regular contact with the Trade Union Movement, raised me above my petty concerns.

SC: In your opinion what are the qualities that writers and intellectuals should cultivate in themselves in order to combat the conspiracies of vested interests and imperialism to create enmity among the people on a linguistic and cultural basis?

FAF: First of all, they should be good intellectuals and writers. Bad writing and undigested ideas have no impact, no matter how good the writer's intentions might be. The writer should be able to analyse and grasp social realities. In other words, to sift the grain from the chaff, the appearance from the reality. The most important thing is to avoid presenting facts from a purely personal and subjective point of view. On the contrary, one should concentrate on the totality of life and overcome its individual limitations. He should be able to say what the people wish to say but cannot put into words. The writer should become the voice of the dumb masses, a voice they recognize as theirs. After all, the people will resolve their problems, not the writer. But writers can at least help to put the problems clearly in front of them.

Ravindra Kalia*

When Faiz came to Allahabad **

Faiz came to Allahabad twice - first in 1957-58 and the last time in 1981. It was during his latter visit that I had the fortune of having an informal and intimate interaction with him. Allahabad University had organised a function in his honour. I do not remember if there happened anything bigger than this, on the university premises, ever. A massive stage was erected on the lawns of Senate House and by evening, the entire ground under the banyan tree was packed with students of the university. It seemed as if all the rickshaws, tongas, scooters, motorcycles and cars were moving in only one direction. There were many traffic jams. The entire city seemed to have turned out towards the university. Mamta and I, somehow reached the venue. When Faiz appeared on the stage, the entire campus reverberated with the sound of clapping. Mahadevi Verma held the reigns of the *mushaira*. Firaq Sahab was unwell so he was lifted and put onto the stage. Along with Faiz, Firaq and Mahadevi Verma there were Upendranath 'Ashq', Professor Aqil Rizvi and Dr. Muhammad Hasan who adorned the stage. Faiz dwelt upon the crucial link between literature and politics, in his speech and said that his only message to the world is, 'fall in love'. Firaq Sahab seemed to be sitting in a trance. Dr Mohammad Hasan, while addressing the gathering, brought the house down, by paraphrasing a famous couplet of Firaq. The original couplet by Firaq, runs along these lines :

> The coming generations will envy you
>
> When it will occur to them that you have seen Firaq

---

* Ravindra Kalia is Director, Bharatiya Jnanpeeth, New Delhi.

** This piece is an English translation of excerpts from Ravindra Kalia's well known work 'Ghalib Chhuti Sharab', 5th Edition, 2006, Vaani Prakashan, New Delhi.

Dr Hasan changed it, to say that coming generations will envy you(the audience) when they realize that you had seen Faiz, Firaq and Mahadevi in flesh and blood.

Faiz had come to Allahabad on the invitation of Prof. Udit Narayan Singh, the then Vice-Chancellor of the university. Though his subject was Mathematics, he had come to develop a keen interest in Urdu poetry, through his interaction, with a young student leader and an Urdu enthusiast Devi Prasad Tripathi (DPT), and could now quote quite a bit of Faiz, extempore. When the proposal to invite Faiz to Allahabad was put before him, he readily agreed.

Faiz spent an entire evening in the company of Hindi writers. Vibhuti Narayan Rai, the then city superintendent of police, was chosen to be the host. Both he and DPT were class fellows.

I must say that there could not have been a better host than him for the occasion. Writers, poets, playwrights, artists from both Urdu and Hindi had assembled there, to soak in the atmosphere, fragrant with the presence of Faiz. It seemed as if a long lost friend had come back after ages, from across many seas and oceans. Every one wanted to hear and record his favourite *ghazal* from Faiz Sahab and he could not say no to anyone.

It will not be out of place to draw attention to the fact that Faiz recited his poetry in a most unimpressive and desultory manner almost as if it was the poetry of an enemy. I have not seen a poet who recited so plainly and with such detachment. When I said this to Doodhnath Singh who was sitting next to me, he spoke like a wise crow, "You are a fool, Kalia! Perhaps you do not know that Ghalib's recitation was even worse. Always remember, the lesser the poet, the better his rendering!"

Faiz was overwhelmed by Allahabad, especially with the feeling that he was equally loved and admired among Hindi writers. If he ever stumbled in his rendering, someone or the other would pop up the missing word and Faiz would pick up from there and continue. Every one in the party was beside himself - some with poetry, some with wine, and others with the sheer magic of the atmosphere.

After some time DPT came and sat at the feet of Faiz Sahab, put his hand over his ear and began to sing an Awadhi folk song with absolute indulgence. This amused Faiz greatly. He also heaved a sigh of relief as he was continuously either reciting his *ghazals,* or saying something or the other.

Eventually the evening came to an end. Everyone ate, got themselves photographed in groups with Faiz and gradually dispersed. DPT came and sat with Faiz Sahab in the car. Faiz Sahab requested him to sing some more folk songs. DPT struck a note again and the car started.

Romonika & Vimlendra Sharan*

My friend, my mate ... Faiz - a poetic journey

This article is not a critique of Faiz or his works. Penned here are my thoughts of an evening, seeped in Faiz...from romance to realism.

Despite a decade in Delhi, the road rage in the morning and the numb dullness of office colleagues, never fail to warp the best and freshest intentions, I start the day with. *Dilli sheher se ishq nahi asaan* - this was the train of thought that wove through the humdrum details of a busy working day as I struggled to retain a work life balance amid encounters with recalcitrant domestic and professional issues.

Today was a specially difficult day as I was trying to organise conflicting demands on time and space to achieve a niche of calm in the evening-a mirage floated somewhere just beyond my reach. I had been promised an evening of Faiz by a Pakistani singer, Tina Sani. Faiz, the name, conjured up nuances, long forgotten in the mists of youthful experiments with poetry and I recalled the trajectory of his art and life, so inextricably linked with the art and history of the subcontinent. Faiz Ahmed Faiz - the voice of the conscience of the suffering humanity of our times.

As I juggled to carve out a space among the fragments of the day, I almost sighed in despair at the madness of the city which engulfed me even as the familiar lines from a Faiz favourite, floated through my mind:

> Messiah of crystals pearl, crystal goblet, once broken is broken
>
> Tears cannot mend it, its lost if broken
>
> You gather the shards, save them for naught

---

* Romonika Sharan is the General Manager, Bharat Sanchar Nigam Ltd (BSNL), New Delhi. Vimlendra Sharan is an Indian Administrative Service (IAS) officer posted in Delhi.

There is no messiah of crystals, what good is your hope?

I wondered, surrounded as I was by *kaanch ke dhaanchey* (fragile goblets/creations of glass] whether it would be possible to move beyond the mere reflections of words and soak in the deeper nuances of poetry, in the evening? Was it the sheer sense of indulgence that led me to abandon routine and plunge into a world of velvet words or was it the opportunity to feel momentarily the pulsating rhythms of revolution and the lilt of love?

I don't know. But the songs of love and anthems of revolution led to one of the best evenings of my life, as the traditional expressions of love got fused with the travails of the afflicted humanity. I lost my soul to the familiar strains of *nazms* and *ghazals* rendered with inimitable finesse and feeling, by the artists for the evening.

A nodding familiarity with the nuances of Urdu and a love of poetry gave us the feeling that we were equipped, for the evening. With Tina Sani approaching the different shades of love and longing, the refreshing dip into past melodies and well loved lyrics like "let clouds gather and some wine flow...let there be anguish...almost a surge of lightning when in front of me, she came unveiled" brought back the innocence and enchantment of new blossomed love and then led us from romance to realism with the strains of "Don't ask me now, Beloved, to love you as I did". A mature acceptance of love at high noon, soon to dip into sunset glories. The waves of socialist and non conformist thought of the Progressive Writers' Association swept over me with the expressive rendition of Faiz -

The world knows pains besides those of love

There are joys besides the joys of our love

The dread spell of countless centuries

Draped in silk, satin, and gold brocade

In those streets and bazaars, everywhere bodies are sold

Besmeared with dirt, bathed in blood

Faiz, with his eclectic background in English and Arabic literature and deep involvement with the voices of dissent in politics, underpinned by his strong commitment to the oppressed classes, was imbued with a deep and abiding humanism, that makes him timeless, even a hundred years after his birth. His opposition to oppression, whether the feudal and colonial miasma or the self inflicted bloodshed of the Bangladesh war, led him to frame a utopian ideal, where he voices the eternal hope of the revolutionary:

> When from the face of God's earth,
> all idols are banished from his house,
> We, the righteous yet downtrodden of the house
> will be catapulted to the highest place;
> Whilst all the crowns are thrown high
> and all the thrones torn down

As these strains of 'Hum Dekhenge' washed over the spell bound audience, they brought to mind the humanism of another great poet and I recalled the heaven of freedom into which Tagore had wanted his country to awake, with a mind without fear and the head held high. I could not help but wonder at the continuing bloodshed in the subcontinent and the world at large and pray, that the immortal verses of these inimitable minds seep into the fabric of each fractured nation and heal the wounded spirits and succour the stifled voices. I wondered how in his days of imprisonment, Faiz too must have gazed at a slice of sky, waiting for some cloud, some hope of rain in a dark continent's wait for change...even today, I mused at the inexplicable opacity of political and military leadership in the subcontinent as the cry, so beautifully articulated by him, becomes a personal statement for so many of the marginalised.

As the evening moved towards its inevitable end, the elegance of the polished verse, deceptively conversational, yet thought provoking and poignant without constraints of time, space and context, caught us all up in an elegiac mood, so elegantly expressed by Gulzar, a day later, at the same venue when he lamented that the crisp sound of a page being turned has increasingly been replaced by the dry click on a keyboard...changing the whole flavour of communication.

Gradually resurfacing to the reality of what TS Eliot called the 'unreal city' of scams and skillful shortcuts in life and relationships, I was reminded of his lines, wondering, "I had not thought death had undone so many". I realised that in this city, one must take grace where one finds it, when one finds it. I moved back into the realm of reality with Faiz:

> The night brought back a long lost memory of yours
>
> The way spring silently surprises a deserted wasteland.

Memory Speaks

Faiz and family in 1955

Faiz on his release from prison, 1955

Sajjad Zaheer*

The Rawalpindi Conspiracy Case

Lucknow, 13 January, 1956

During the period of the Rawalpindi Conspiracy Case, Faiz and I were together in the Central Jail, Hyderabad, Sindh. In December 1952, the hearing of our case had come to an end. We, no longer, had to appear for interminable hours, day after day, in the stand for the accused, and were thus spared the statements of witnesses, the questionings and arguments of lawyers, and the legal hair- splittings of the learned judges. The judgment had not yet been passed, and so we were in a state of suspended hope.

It was at this time that we received news of the publication of "Dast-e-Saba". We had of course heard all the poems recited by Faiz, and had read them many times over, but nevertheless, those of us who were inclined towards literature, were overjoyed. After getting the required permission from the jail authorities, we organised a party in which all the prisoners congratulated Faiz, on the publication of his book. On this occasion I said that many years from now, when people will have forgotten all about the Rawalpindi Conspiracy Case, and Pakistani historians write about the noteworthy events of 1952, then the publication of this slim volume of verse will be counted as the year's most significant happening.

A great deal has been said by both well-wishers as well as hostile critics in recent times about the decline in importance of the Progressive Writers' Movement, and of Urdu literature in general, but I disagree with such a stance. In fact, I believe that the current state of Urdu literature is indeed extremely bright. This era begins around 1930, and continues up to the present moment. If we consider the past four or five years, and examine Faiz's 'Dast-e-Saba' and 'Zindaan Nama', Ehtesham Hussain's

* Late Sajjad Zaheer, a celebrated litterateur, was one of the founder members of Progressive Writers' Association of India.

Faiz Ahmed Faiz and Sajjad Zaheer

'Tanqeed aur Amali Tanqeed', Nadeem Qasmi's 'Shola-e-Gul', Sardar Jafri's 'Pathar Ki Deewar' and Majnun Gorakhpuri's 'Naqoosh-o-Afkar', among other works, we can state with confidence that the red flame of creative activity burns brightly amidst the storms of ignorance and backwardness. These storms activate it to such an extent that the flame's truth assumes an ever brighter appearance, and its beauty and influence is permeated with hundreds of new shades.

Faiz wrote most of the poems contained in "Zindaan Nama" during his incarceration, in Montgomery Central Jail (now Sahiwal), and Lahore Central Jail, between July 1953 and March 1955. During this period we were separated, as both of us had been dealt sentences of four years hard labour each, and were dispatched to different jails. Faiz was sent to Sahiwal Jail in the Punjab and I was sent to Central Jail in Baluchistan. We could not correspond with one another, but through the letters of friends and in certain Urdu journals I was able to read some of the *ghazals* of Faiz, during this period.

Nowadays, (in 1956), I am leading a pleasant existence in a free environment, yet when I remember the mental, emotional and spiritual condition of those jail days, when I used to immerse myself in the poetry of my dearest friend and beloved comrade, I find it difficult to describe my feelings adequately. Perhaps too much emotion is unsuitable for detached criticism. Many of our experiments, our dreams, our loves and hates, and our plans, regarding the bringing of beauty and fruitfulness to our own two countries, were identical. That is why I was exceptionally moved by Faiz's poetry of this period.

Sometimes my heart bled because of having had to suffer the travails of incarceration, which, in Faiz, produced such generosity of spirit. I was filled with wonder at this aspect of his creativity, and at the manner in which he expressed the most noble of emotions, which blazed forth like the rays of the sun.

If we look at these poems of Faiz in totality, we realise that as far as his beliefs are concerned, they are similar to those which all progressive writers consider to be their basic tenets. Yet in Faiz's poetry, these values are presented in the most unique and musical manner possible. His imagery contains within it, the very essence of our countries' existence, and its democratic aims which shine forth, from our best minds.

His poetry embodies the basic requirements of a civilized existence, in which both the body and the spirit are nurtured in equal proportions. I believe that this is the secret of his popularity in both India and Pakistan. His admirers now expect that after 'Naqsh-e-Fariadi', 'Dast-e-Saba' and 'Zindaan Nama', Faiz will progress further and produce poetry of greater value and significance.

Source: Two Loves - Faiz's Letters from Jail, Eds. Kyala Pasha & Salima Hashmi, Published by Sang-e-Meel Publications, Lahore, Pakistan

Salima Hashmi*

A summer in Beirut with Abbu

In the summer of 1980, having received a wistful letter from my father, I determined to take my children, Yasser, aged 11, and Mira, 6, to visit my parents in Beirut. Being an employee of the Government, this involved a series of forays into various departments to elicit the coveted 'No Objection Certificate' or NOC, as it is tenderly termed. From Education to Culture, to the dreaded Ministry of Interior, I made the rounds, chatting up section officers, deputy secretaries and occasionally *chaprasis*, to move the 'file' along the corridors of power. The final denouement was in the office of the all powerful, all knowing Federal Secretary of the Ministry of Interior, a seasoned civil servant, who in his more benign incarnation, claimed to be a friend of Faiz, and was now General Zia ul Haq's omnipresent eyes and ears.

As I sat before him, to beg for my clearance to leave the country, we chitchatted light heartedly about everything but the purpose of my visit, which sat like a large, dark shape between us. Once or twice he made an oblique reference to why his friend lived in Beirut, a city torn apart by violent conflict, where I was now taking my children. I, equally obtuse, spoke of one's reasons for travel and reunions. As I watched the stamp of approval come down on the paper, I could not resist telling him that things at home were not quite as calm as he supposed. My parting promise was to convey his affectionate greetings to his dear friend in Beirut.

A week later, I watched my children faces light up with curiosity and excitement as the plane touched down at Beirut Airport. I had already shed a tear in expectation of seeing my father's face after more than two

---

* Salima Hashmi, elder daughter of Faiz Ahmed Faiz, is the Dean, School of Visual Arts and Design, Beaconhouse National University, Lahore, Pakistan.

years of separation. Even in his years in jail, we had met every six months or so.

Beirut Airport was chaotic and we couldn't find him. A few phone calls later, he located us and we were on our way, interrupted by road blocks, military searches and vast potholes.

All this I recalled recently, rummaging through a pile of photographs, thumbed through diaries, used airline tickets, and crumpled shopping lists from our 'Beirut Summer'. I also found the notes for an article, never written. So here goes:

'In memory of the Summer of 1980'

People ask "what is Faiz doing in Beirut?" and to see for myself, this summer I decided to find out what Faiz is doing in this turbulent hub of the Arab world.

In a tiny 6th floor flat in the Raouche section of Beirut, Faiz lives with his wife. It is a quiet, ordered existence. His 'office', the editorial section of the Afro-Asian Journal *Lotus* is across the corridor from his flat, with the Arabic language Lotus office two doors away. The chief editorship of *Lotus* was unanimously offered to Faiz by the Afro-Asian Writers' Union more than a year ago, and Faiz accepted the offer as an acknowledgment of the recognition of Pakistani writers. The headquarters of *Lotus* was shifted from Cairo after Anwar Saadat's defection to the American camp, seen as betrayal of the Arab cause. *Lotus* found a home and hospitality in Beirut from the Union of Palestinian Writers. Faiz is now trying to revive and revitalise *Lotus*, whose first issue under his editorship, appeared last month in English, French and Arabic editions. He is in contact with writers' organisations, book shops, librarians and universities all over the world, trying to interest them in new Afro-Asian writings. His small office now receives enquiries and literary contributions from all over the world. As I lounged on his sofa, an article on a Filipino painter arrived in the mail, together with new poems from Syria, a story from Korea, an order for a hundred copies of the French edition from Ethiopia, and a request for the Arabic edition from Kuwait. And so Faiz is keeping busy, giving the journal shape, arranging for translators, writing letters and having discussion sessions with his small staff.

But if one were to ask "Is Faiz happy there?" The answer is all too apparent every evening, when he steps out alone and strolls along the once elegant Raouché district, where militia men guard every apartment building, and refugee children play in the door-ways. Faiz walks here at dusk, smoking his perennial cigarette. More often than not, he spends the rest of the evening on the balcony of the flat, over looking the sea. His sadness and his longing for home is a solid concrete wall which blocks his view. This has been the main spring for his latest poetry which has been coming and is furious almost like his prison poetry. His new collection is now complete, poems written after his departure from home in the spring of 1978. Faiz has named the book 'Mere dil, mere musafir' and it will be published early in 1981, in time for his 70th birthday.

During his two years abroad, Faiz has travelled a great deal. Invitations have come from all over the world; from Hawaii, from Bulgaria, from Canada and from USA, from Korea and from Angola. He is, these days, attending an Afro-Asian Writers' meet in Mongolia, from where he goes to London on invitation of the 3rd World Foundation, who are releasing a long-playing record of Faiz's poetry. Then to Canada for a Mushaira and back to Beirut to prepare the next issue of *Lotus*.

Faiz, when I left him, had just recovered from a bronchial infection, and had been ordered yet again by the doctor to cut down on his smoking.

The Arab literary world is highly inbred and although they accord Faiz great respect, this is not his scene. He misses his 'yaars', his milieu. However, he has time to read, go to the cinema, (something he never had time for) listen to music and of course to write. His occasional visitors are Palestinian, Syrian and Lebanese writers or the few Pakistanis who remain in this politically unpredictable city. The thing that strikes one about Beirut is that life goes on. The newest cars jam streets, glossy people fill the restaurants, and money flows ostentatiously and endlessly. A bomb goes off in the neighborhood, streets are closed as machine guns rattle, ambulance sirens scream, and then business is as usual. And in the midst of this microcosm of the Middle-East conflict and Arab politics, Faiz, quietly goes about his work and makes poetry.

Moneeza Hashmi*

What's in a name ... unless it is Faiz!

I don't recall when exactly I became aware of the fact that my father was a famous or for others an "infamous" man. Growing up for me, as I look back was perhaps somewhat normal, given the circumstances. We got up in the morning and went to school first on the handle bar of a servant's bicycle then progressed to a *tonga* (a horse driven carriage) and then to a car. Mama would be around to send us off to school. She would not be present when we returned but would arrive later huffing and puffing, depending on the weather and her own day spent in the office. She would cycle to office and so would be tired and somewhat edgy, on her return. Our caretaker was a wizened old servant who was the butler, bearer, confidante, whatever.

I never remember actually noticing or commenting on the absence of an important person missing from this small group. Abbu, as we called our father, was not physically present, while I was growing up but his aura was definitely around us. Our frequent visits to meet him in jail, are etched so clearly in my mind and yet I cannot recall thinking of him as having done something seriously wrong or criminal, to have ended up there. I would ceaselessly ask when he would come home but never why he was away from us. Perhaps somewhere in the corner of my mind I had tucked away the reason and since I did not understand at the time, all of what the actual connotations were, it just stayed curled up somewhere in the recesses of my mind gathering "dust." For me, the happy moments were the jail visits because I always had to take time off from school!

But I was very much aware that there was a person who was not

---

* Moneeza Hashmi, younger daughter of Faiz Ahmed Faiz, is the President, Commonwealth Broadcasting Association, London, United Kingdom (UK).

physically present but very much a part of our daily lives and whose name was intertwined with mine. How much weight that name carried would become more and more apparent as I grew up.

There was that time, a few years after his death when I was standing at the tomb of a poet in Tajikistan and since I have been brought up in the tradition of offering *fateha* at graves, with my head covered, I was doing that when I felt a tap on my shoulder. I turned around to see a bus load of local inhabitants smiling and wanting to shake my hand. Somewhat unnerved at this public response of affection from total strangers, I asked my interpreter Natasha, what it was all about. She said,"They were curious to know who was this strangely dressed person. I told them you are the daughter of Faiz and they all wanted to pay their respects". There was no communication between us but their warmth is still etched in my heart and imprinted on my mind. Each and every one of them shook my hand and said words of welcome and sent greetings to my family and country. That was the magic of the name I am blessed with.

And then there is the time, when, due to unpleasant circumstances and other political repercussions, I, as an employee of Pakistan Television found myself facing a 4 star serving army general, who was heading the Information and Broadcasting Ministry in the Martial Law era of General Zia ul Haq. The employees union at the time had "taken over" the PTV premises, which were then "taken back" by the army and we, senior employees were facing the brunt of the wrath of the dictator. We had not been consulted about this extremely rash step, taken by the union office bearers and had been circumstantially coerced against our will, to be locked out of the premises, as the army moved in to run the television transmission. When tempers cooled down and a "cease fire" was announced by both sides, the witch hunting began. I, being a senior and well respected member of the management cadre, at the time, was being questioned about my role in the so called "revolt" of the employees. The general heading the inquiry committee, gave me a few minutes to say my piece. After hearing me out somewhat impatiently he looked at me, from above his horn rimmed spectacles and said,"You do know you are the daughter of Faiz Ahmed Faiz?" What he meant by that question, I never found out because I did not blink an eye lid when I answered, "It's too late to change my father or my name", and walked out.

If I was going to lose my job because of my name, so be it. I didn't, as it turned out and went on to achieve a long and successful career in the media, with which I am still associated today, 40 years down the line.

On yet another occasion, I was standing before a complete stranger in a foreign embassy, on whose judgement depended my visa status for the next five years. She asked me the required mundane questions but lastly as she flicked through my passport pages she found my recent frequent visits to India intriguing. "I am being invited to speak at events being organised for my father" was my answer to her quizzical expression." And what does he do?" she wanted to know. "Did. He wrote poetry. He passed away many years ago," I answered, hoping to close the conversation. It had been an early haul to the embassy and I wanted to go back to my missed cup of tea.

"His name?" she asked, as she hammered away at the key board.

"Faiz" I made it short.

Her fingers stopped typing in mid air.

I thought maybe she hadn't heard me."Faiz. Faiz Ahmed Faiz" I repeated a little more loudly.

Now she turned to look at me and gave me a full face stare. "Lady, I should be asking for your autograph not interviewing you. I have a celebrity standing right here". A smile and then she turned back to start typing again. Needless to add, I walked out with a 5 year visa status!

And then there have been umpteen times, when I have walked into a room, full of complete strangers, who have stood up in awe because of my parentage. I have sat down with influential people in a foreign country, to talk business and suddenly somewhere someone has said the magic name and the entire atmosphere has become soft, his verses start making the rounds and I am given more respect than I deserve or than when I came into the room.

I walk in the park and hear "Faiz's daughter" whispered almost every single day, as people pass by. I go to the local grocery shop and meet a total stranger who shares memories with me. I meet so many icons, role models, people I admire and before I can begin telling them how pleased I am to meet them face to face, their expressions tell me, it is they who are pleased to meet the daughter of Faiz. And I am humbled beyond words.

I have shaken hands with Presidents, Prime Ministers, Kings and Queens. Each time, stealing a little glory by ensuring subtly each time that they found out about my parentage! It always brought an extra smile or raised an eye brow as I walked away.

So what's in a name? Nothing much really. Unless of course it happens to be Faiz!

Ali Madeeh Hashmi*

My grandfather was a treasure of pain

Strangers spared no arrows of abuse / Lovers, no style of reproach ... ***Faiz Ahmed Faiz.***

"Do you also write poetry?" is a question often asked of us, perhaps with the assumption that something of Faiz's genius may have trickled down into his family. Sadly our answer is always no. Poets have always been a breed apart. Altaf Hussain 'Hali' in his seminal 'Muqaddama Shair-o Shaaeri' (Foreword of Poetry) quotes an unnamed poet, as saying that there was no occupation more degrading than poetry. In ancient Greece, Plato drew up an outline of a democratic government in which every occupation was represented, except that of a poet. On the other hand, good poets have been hailed and admired as visionaries, ahead of their time and their eras. These ideas reach their contradictory apogee with the elevation of great poets to the ranks of fortune tellers and sooth sayers, voices in the dark that can lead people towards a goal, that few can even imagine, let alone see. In ancient Arabia, 'Kahins' were 'a group of cultic officials...poets who primarily functioned as soothsayers and, for a fee, would fall into a trance, in which they would reveal divine messages, through rhyming couplets'. The enemies of the prophet of Islam, Muhammad, accused him of being a 'Kahin' and would ask mockingly "Should we abandon our gods for the sake of an insane poet?" (The Quran 37:36). The fact that there are dozens of verses in the Quran, refuting the accusation that Muhammad was a 'Kahin' reveals how sensitive this issue was.

In the Middle Ages, the poetry of Hafez of Shiraz, the 'poet of poets' was often used in ancient Persia to predict fortunes. Mirza Ghalib, that genius of India, wrote, "They descend from the unseen, these words/Ghalib,

* Dr. Ali Madeeh Hashmi is a psychiatrist based in Lahore, Pakistan.

the scratching of the pen is the voice of angels". Sigmund Freud, the founder of modern psychoanalysis wrote, 'everywhere I go, a poet has been there before me'.

Is it any wonder that the descendants of Faiz would hesitate to go where angels fear to tread? Faiz himself once described how verses came to him, how he would feel a strange lightness, how the sky and the horizon would seem like it had changed colours and he would know that a poem was about to be born. Of course, none of this 'unseen, hidden' business would have meant a thing if Faiz did not have a solid foundation in the literature and poetry of his era. By all accounts, he had been a voracious reader since a young age and extremely intellectually gifted. This he probably inherited from his father, Sultan Mohammad Khan, who rose from being a village shepherd to a minister in the Afghan King's government and later a Cambridge educated lawyer. Faiz polished his gifts, by choosing to study languages and literature in college and later adopting journalism (and trade unionism) as his career. His meeting with Sajjad Zaheer and his involvement in the All India Progressive Writers' Association, shaped his subsequent political ideals and his work.

2011 is Faiz's Centennial, 100 years since his birth. What is his legacy 100 years after he was born and more than 25 years after his death? Should an artist such as a poet, be judged solely on the merit of his art or his social and political involvement?

Already, in the span of a few years, the political ideals he espoused have changed beyond recognition. The great debates of the 20th century, Capitalism vs. Socialism, Colonialism vs. Freedom, First vs. Third world are still with us, albeit in different forms. It is no longer easy to pick sides; perhaps it never was. Faiz's poetic genius though, while shaped and guided by his ideals, was firmly grounded in the classical traditions of Urdu poetry. He used all the allusions and images from the great poets of days gone by, but put them to the service of new social and political ideals. However, Faiz never allowed his verses to become mere political slogans and never compromised his aesthetics for the sake of political expediency. It also goes without saying that he held steadfast throughout his life to the ideals of Progressive Writers' Movement: devotion to the concerns of ordinary workers, peasants, women and the persecuted. It is precisely because he never sloganeered for these ideals though, that his poetry is now recited and read in all manner of gathering of all political shades from the far left to the far right and everyone in between.

We, the family of Faiz, have watched, bemused, while his verses are read aloud by all sides, in all kinds of debates. Faiz would have liked this though. He has been called many things, 'socialist' 'communist' 'atheist' by both his detractors and admirers, but ultimately he was a man beyond labels. His philosophy rises above these ideological restrictions. He was, in the best sense of the word, an inclusive humanist, someone who identified with and embraced all that was good in all of us. In his speech after accepting the Lenin Peace Prize, the former Soviet Union's equivalent of the Nobel Peace Prize in 1962, he said: "A few days ago, when the echoes of the latest Soviet accomplishment were reverberating across the skies (Faiz is referring here to Yuri Gagarin's orbit around the Earth, the first ever for a human), the thought occurred to me repeatedly that today, when we can observe our world while sitting amongst the stars, these petty conflicts, this selfishness of trying to divide pieces of our planet into parts and trying to lord it over groups of people, how all of this seems beyond reason. Today, the highways of the universe are open to us. When all the treasures of the world are in our grasp, are there not a few intelligent, justice loving and honest people in this world who can convince the rest to wrap up these military bases, sink all these bombs, rockets, cannons and guns into the sea and instead of trying to subjugate one another, set out together to conquer the universe, where there is no shortage of space, where no one needs to fight another, where there are unlimited skies and innumerable worlds? I am certain that despite our problems and obstacles, we will be able to convince our human fraternity of this".

For Faiz, everyone, including those who considered him an enemy, 'the most dangerous communist of his time' were worthy of respect and affection. This of course, is a quintessentially *Sufi* ideal, the fact that everything in this universe is but a reflection of the Divine and sings its praise. Faiz himself referred to this when he told his translator and friend, the eminent American poet Naomi Lazard that the true subject of poetry is always the loss of the beloved (in Sufi thought, the true Beloved, of course, is always the Divine, to which all return). Faiz, even at his most passionate, never advocated violence.

Is it desirable though to walk this path? Is it even possible? To struggle but never fight; to hold fast to a principle and yet not be dogmatic? To see injustice, pain and violence and all the things that make one's blood boil around you and yet keep a smile on one's lips? To allow oneself to become so indifferent to worldly needs that one has nothing that anyone can threaten to take away? Faiz thought so. After all, it was Faiz himself who wrote in one of his last poems, a Persian *Na'at* (Ode to the Prophet):

> 'The rulers on their thrones are slaves to anxieties of land and wealth
>
> Upon the dusty earth, Oh envy of the rulers of the age is thy mendicant!'

But what good did all this do him? What difference does it make? Shouldn't people who want to make a difference be manning a barricade somewhere in Tahrir Square and fighting off the forces of a vicious State? Isn't there something more worthwhile than writing, that we all should be doing in order to correct all the injustice and oppression in the world? What good is writing, or poetry, or painting or music in this messed up world? Aren't all these just excuses for dilettantes to avoid the 'real' work? Faiz himself answered this in 'The Role of the Artist', a brief essay first published in *The Ravi*, the literary magazine of Lahore's prestigious Government College, his alma mater:

> Who are we, the writer, poets and artists and what can we contribute to avert the mortal calamities threatening mankind? My answer is that we are the offspring, in the direct line of descent of the magicians and the sorcerers and music makers of old. In times gone by, these ancient ancestors of ours could make the rain come down with their incantations and with their songs could make the deserts bloom. This is because they found for the hopes and fears of their people, for their dreams and longings, words and music that they could not find for themselves.

Elsewhere he writes:

> Literature, like science, is a social activity. The result of every scientific discovery (has been) some transformation in the social life of man. Literature unfolds in a similar fashion...the unexplored or dimly felt complexities of social reality, the given human situation of a given time. The impact of (the writer) on his social universe, however, is more insidious, more subtle and the same time more direct than the work of his scientific colleagues. The scientist may claim with some justification that he could not foresee the practical or social consequences of a mathematical equation he formulated. The writer can plead no such alibi. His work is deliberately manipulative and formative of the consciousness of the audience for whom he writes... A physical scientist will not deliberately seek to ignore or falsify the known facts of physical reality. A writer, however, may be tempted, coerced or bribed (to do so).

I never knew him very well while he was alive. He was too busy travelling and working. Even when he was at home, his wide circle of friends and admirers rarely allowed us grandchildren, any time with him. How does one begin to take the measure of a man who realised himself more fully than many can ever dream of? A man who 'walked with kings and never lost his common touch'?

Faiz spoke of social justice but without violence, of struggle without anger. Does this point of view have a place in the world today when, once again, ideological battle lines are being drawn ever more sharply? Faiz would have been happy to see the backs of Ben Ali of Tunisia, Mubarak of Egypt and Gaddafi of Libya but most likely he would have composed a hymn of sadness for all those who fell in the battles. He would have exhorted the 'wretched of the Earth' to 'claw away the mask of pain from their eyes' and 'come, like the lion'. He may have decided that he needed to be in the midst of all those struggling to shatter the 'bestial spells of countless centuries' and might have gone to live in Cairo or Tunis or Benghazi. Most definitely, he would have advised the people of those lands to not let their fate be decided by others. He would have beseeched them to make their own fate with their own hands.

We, at Faiz Foundation/Faiz Ghar are proud to own and uphold the legacy of Faiz. Faiz Ghar (www.faizghar.net) a small museum and library in Lahore was set up two years ago, expressly for the purpose of carrying Faiz's message of social justice, humanism and peace forward, for coming generations. This year his Centennial is being celebrated all over the world, including in India which held a special place of affection in Faiz's heart.

We invite all those who share Faiz's ideals, to join hands with us and 'Walk on, that destination is not here yet'.

Mira Hashmi*

A tribute from granddaughter

Since I was a little girl, I've repeatedly been asked the question 'what is it like, being Faiz's granddaughter?' Though in reply, I usually just smile a knowing, somewhat smart-ass-ish smile with a hint of self-deprecation, in my head I'm often thinking, to paraphrase Carrie Fisher, 'well, compared to what? When I wasn't his granddaughter?' That's a tough one because I've been that for as long as I can remember, which is a fairly long time, and since my mother is older than me and her father was quite a bit older than her, it's fairly safe to say, I think, that it would be quite inconceivable for me to have awareness of a period in which I was not his granddaughter, but something or someone else. And not knowing what it might be like to not be his granddaughter, it's rather difficult for me to say what it's been like to be his granddaughter. I suppose I should probably, at some point, sit down and think of a suitably reverent and wise-sounding stock answer, but, I must confess, it's not a subject I like to actively ponder over, for fear of feeling, well, like the runt of the litter, to be perfectly honest. Oh I haven't done that badly for myself of course, but comparisons, even if they are imagined rather than explicitly expressed, can be daunting. That's actually the reason, I pretty much gave up writing poetry after my poem 'I have a cat, his name is Pat' which I composed while a student of Class 4; though it was favourably received, I didn't see it standing up too well against the likes of *Aaj Baazar Mein Pa-bajaulaan Chalo* et al.

It was around the same time that he passed away, barely a year after returning to his homeland after a long time spent in self-imposed exile. He had lived for a number of years in the Lebanese capital of Beirut, as the editor of the literary magazine *Lotus*, where, in the summer of 1980, I went to visit him and *Mama* (Alys) accompanied by my mother and elder brother Yasser. I was six (the age my own son is now) and the most vivid memories I have of that period of my life are of the time I spent in Beirut

---

* Mira Hashmi is a film maker based in Lahore, Pakistan.

with my grandparents. I remember their small but cosy and welcoming apartment on the sixth floor with its tiny balcony out front, looking onto the Mediterranean Sea, where Nana would sit in the evenings. The kitchen was the tiniest I'd ever seen, and the bathroom faucets gave out salt-water. *Nana* had in his employ, a handsome chauffeur called Musa, and Rita, his secretary, with whom I liked to hang around because she was so pretty, and funny as well. On Sundays, *Mama* would cook us two kids sausages and chips which we would devour while watching 'The Incredible Hulk' on TV.

Nana would spend most of the day in his office, which was housed in an apartment across the hall from the one which housed his home, an ideal commute! There was plenty of paper for me to draw on which Rita, very generously handed out, whenever I requested. With Rita clacking away on her typewriter in the back office, *Nana* would sit at his roomy desk, and I would be sprawled on the carpeted floor near him, doodling away all day. Once *Nana* asked me to ask Rita if his coffee was ready. By that time in his life, his incessant smoking had turned his voice a bit gruff and I thought he'd said 'ask Rita if my copy is ready.' I went off dutifully to enquire after the said copy. Of course poor Rita had no clue what I was talking about. "Copy of what?", she asked, looking puzzled. I didn't have the answer to that so I just repeated the question more forcefully, at which point I heard *Nana* in the other room, first chuckling and then roaring with laughter, having overheard my snippet of mis-communication.

I'm sure a lot of people find it hard to imagine *Nana* laughing out loud like that; some would be surprised to know he had a sharp sense of humour and that he enjoyed an off-colour joke as much as the next person. But that's the wonderful thing, isn't it? One is always surprised by new discoveries about those we love and admire. Like my surprise, when his funeral was attended by hundreds of people, including so many faces I'd seen on TV and in magazines; when condolence messages came from all over the world from all sorts of people, including Sunil Dutt and Dilip Kumar. That was one of the first inklings for me that he was much more than just my *Nana.* And I'm still getting to know him.

So what's it like to be his granddaughter? I could try to say something profound here, but suffice to say: Nice. Really, really nice.

Amrita Pritam* in conversation with Alys Faiz

Faiz was true to his art, to his character and creativity ...

Amrita Pritam: Alys, where did you meet Faiz Sahab for the first time? In your own country England?

Alys: No, my sister was married in India to one Dr. Taseer, they had met in London; and, incidentally, in 1938, I had come to India to meet her.

Amrita: So you saw India in the form of Faiz Sahab?

Alys: Yes, I met him in Amritsar; Amritsar became India, and India was Faiz Sahab.

Amrita: You did not know Urdu, so how could his Urdu poetry strike you?

Alys: Amrita, the truth is I have not yet fathomed the depths of his Urdu poetry; learning a language and being able to read and speak in that language is one thing, but understanding the whole culture and being at one with it, is quite different.

Amrita: Then you loved Faiz the person, not Faiz the poet?

Alys: Yes, but since poetry is part of the personality, and one has to live life with that person, so one has to know many things, which I did endeavour to know.

Amrita: How long was the courtship before marriage came?

Alys: Nearly two years, and it prolonged as much because consent of the parents (of Faiz Sahab) was required. We did not want to marry unless the family atmosphere was congenial.

Amrita : Where was the marriage arranged and solemnized?

---

* Late Amrita Pritam- a much celebrated writer.

Alys: Kashmir. Maharaja of Kashmir gave us his summer palace and Sheikh Abdullah solemnized our marriage.

Amrita: And the *barat* (marriage party) came from Lahore?

Alys: Yes, it was a three people *barati* - Faiz, his elder brother, and his friend Naeem. After they arrived, the first thing that I asked Faiz Sahab was, "Have you brought the marriage ring or not?" Faiz said, "I have brought the ring and I have brought the saree, too." I was surprised as to how could he have gotten the size for my ring! When I asked him, he said,"I bought on my size."

Amrita Pritam : Faiz Sahab must have presumed that when hearts have matched, fingers, too, would match. Now, you tell me if there was a *mushaira* (poetry recital) to celebrate your marriage?

Alys: Yes, there was one. First we had dinner with Sheikh Abdullah and his wife, and then the *mushaira* took place. Majaz and Josh Malihabadi were also present.

Amrita: When did you meet his (Faiz Sahab) relatives?

Alys: We stayed in Kashmir for three days and then came to Lahore where *Dawat-e-Walima* (feast to celebrate marriage) was given.

Amrita : How did you take the blessings of your mother-in-law?

Alys : I drew *ghoonghat* (part of saree) over my head and bowed.

Amrita : Oh, really! Is it true! Was there a proper ritual to unveil you?

Alys : Yes, Amrita! I was blessed and given silver coins.

Amrita : Your mother-in-law did not change your name?

Alys : She did. She named me 'Kulsum.' But I did not like the name.

Amrita : When did you learn Urdu?

Alys : I learnt it at home from his (Faiz Sahab) nephew. I taught him English and learnt Urdu from him.

Amrita: When was his first poetry collection 'Naqsh-e-Fariadi' published? Was it published by then?

Faiz Ahmed Faiz and Alys Faiz

Alys : Yes, perhaps it was published a year ago.

Amrita : Did Faiz recount to you his earlier love affairs about whom there are *nazms* (verses) in 'Naqsh-e-Fariadi?'

Alys: Yes, Amrita! Not only those, he shared with me his later friendships, too. But they had no impact on my life, none at all. Faiz is a rock in himself - he is loyal to his art, to his pen and paper.

Amrita: You are right! If someone is true to his art, to his character and creativity, who could be more loyal and trustworthy than him?

Alys : Thirty seven years have passed in between since we got married.

Amrita: How has been the fusion of East and West in your case?

Alys: I must say that when two people from different and unlike cultures marry then, I think, it becomes difficult for the man to live in the woman's country, but the woman can adjust in her man's country because women have the strength and capacity to adapt to the new atmosphere in a foreign land. Marriage between people from different cultures does not work easily.

Amrita: How many children do you have? Two?

Alys: Two daughters - Salima and Moneeza. Salima is a painter and Moneeza is a TV producer. Both are married in the same Punjabi family to two brothers. They live together with their mother-in-law.

Amrita: Alys, you must have translated his (Faiz's) verses into English?

Alys: No, others have done it. A book of translated verses had come some five years ago, which was commissioned by UNESCO.

Amrita: When was Lenin Prize given to Faiz Sahab?

Alys: In 1962 Faiz had a heart-attack; though he had begun to improve, but he was not out of bed-rest yet when the phone from *Pakistan Times* came.

Amrita: What were the first words of Faiz Sahab when he heard the news?

Alys: He became silent. Perhaps he was overwhelmed.

Amrita: What were people's reactions?

Alys: That Faiz should not take this prize, but a telegram from Ayub Khan came, giving him the permission that he can take the prize, there were other such telegrams that we received; then friends started coming to congratulate. Now, the problem was how he would endure the journey to Moscow. Doctors had advised him against air travel, so he took one of the daughters along and went from Lahore to Karachi, by road. From there he sailed up to Naples, and from Naples again by road, up to Moscow.

Amrita: Alys, have you ever thought of writing his (Faiz Sahab) biography?

Alys: Not me, but Zafarul Hasan, in Karachi, is writing it. I think Faiz himself should do it. There is one more thing which is incomplete. Faiz and Sufi Tabassum were together doing translation of Persian Poetry into Urdu. Sufi Tabassum died and Faiz became extremely sad ... that is one important work which is incomplete, and then there are other works also.

Amrita: Yes, Alys. But the most important work above all is to keep Faiz safe.

Alys: Yes, may God protect him!

[Translation from Urdu to English : Sanjeev Ranjan]

Iftikhar Arif and Ahmed Faraz*

Lost opprtunities that Faiz missed all his life ...

Iftikhar Arif : Faiz Sahab, we wanted to converse with you, to interview you , can you tell us the kind of questions we should not ask you?

Faiz : There are many such things; for example, I would definitely not like to be asked about the affairs that are attributed to my name ... besides that I do not know of anything that I would like to hide from you because my life has been like an open book.

Iftikhar Arif : There is general impression that you have lived an extremely luxurious life and that you have enjoyed your success, full throttle. You must have had some regrets, too?

Faiz : One such regret that I can recall is that when I was in school I had this ambition of becoming a famous cricketer. Even now there are moments when I dream that I have become a great test-cricketer and I am playing cricket matches ... but I could not become one. This is one big regret.

Ahmed Faraz: Faiz Sahab, I would like to suggest with utmost humility that even if you had realised your dream and become a famous cricketer and had played for a certain period, would you have, after retirement from cricket, come back to what you have done and are doing?

Faiz: This is hypothetical, isn't it?

Ahmed Faraz : This I said keeping in mind London and England ...

Faiz: As for England I can say that I had taken admission in Cambridge

---

* Iftikhar Arif is the Chairman, Muqtadra Quami Zaban, National Language Authority, Islamabad and a famous poet of Pakistan.

Late Ahmed Faraz was an eminent Urdu poet of Pakistan.

some six months before the World War II began. I was through with all my preparations to go there, my seat was booked in an Italian ship and I was all set to sail. I had even gotten some clothes stitched. This was the period when I taught in a college in Amritsar. I was captain of the college cricket team. There was a Sardarji who used to supply cricketing gear to the team. I had planned that I would find some part-time work there, to take care of my expenses. Sardarji asked me to become his agent and assured me that I would earn a decent commission on whatever he imported from there. But there was a hitch, the Sardarji said that he consults his astrologer before every new venture and that I will have to meet his astrologer. So we went to meet him. After asking me to give him my name and my date of birth he studied my palm and said, "You are not going anywhere ." I said, "What do you mean?" He said, "All routes are closed." I asked him, "What do you mean by 'all routes are closed.' I have the ticket in my pocket, I have already taken admission there, I am all ready to sail." He said, "whether you believe me or not, you are not going anywhere." And eventually his words came true - after a few months, World War II broke out, the Italian ship which was supposed to take us to London did not reach Bombay, and this was how all our routes were actually closed. Since then till date there are moments when I think that there must also be some truth in this system of knowledge.

Ahmed Faraz : Faiz Sahab, I would like to ask you if astrology or power of stars have any place in the purpose of life that you uphold in your literature and discussions? To what extent has that little incident impacted your life?

Faiz : It impacted only to the extent that his words came true. There are times when random predictions hit jackpot.

Iftikhar Arif : Your home was Sialkot, you had your primary education there, could you take us down memory lane, when you were a child there?

Faiz : Childhood memories meaning when I became conscious of my surroundings, which means when I was five, six or seven years old - that was the time when I began memorising the Quran. A Hafiz Sahab was deputed to help me memorise the Quran. I memorised three *siparas* (sections) but my eyes could not endure any further. So that regret is of course there that I could not memorise more. Initially I learnt Urdu and

Persian at home from Master Ata Muhammad. Later I was sent to a *madarsa*. Since Abba (father) happened to be the President of Anjuman Islamia so I was first sent there. Elaborate arrangements were made for my first day to the *madarsa*. I was adorned with velvet clothes, kajal was applied in my eyes, there were many such things that were done and then I was put in a carriage driven by two horses and taken to the *madarsa*. When I reached there I saw poor children in dirty clothes sitting on jute mattresses, spread over the floor. They looked at me with gaping eyes as to see who this new creature was.

Ahmed Faraz : (bowing head in acknowledgment)I must say this had a great impact on Faiz Sahab's life.

Faiz : Children laughed at me with such abandon that I felt extremely ridiculed. I took the vow that from that day onwards I would not do anything that separated me from rest of the children. But I did not stay in that school for long. Children there, made my life hell. Also, since Abba was chairman of the school, every teacher saluted me. There used to be no examination or any such things. Moreover, the Urdu and Persian that I had learnt at home was more than what the teachers at the school knew. So I told Abba one day that I would not go to that school, and from then, I went to a 'mission school.'

This was the time when Congress and Khilafat movements had started. Amritsar was put under Martial Law. The whole atmosphere was stirred up and abuzz with political activities. Leaders from outside used to come and to welcome them, gates laden with flowers used to be erected all over the city. Motor carriages used to be decorated with flowers to carry them. When processions came out, Hindus, Muslims, Sikhs, all came together and raised slogans - *Jo bole so nihal, sat sri akal*, then the takbir *Allah-o-Akbar*, and then the national slogan *Bande Mataram*. In the end there used to be collective singing of Allama Iqbal's tarana *sare jahan se achcha hindustan hamara.*

Such agitations were a common feature those days. Since Abba was a high profile elite of the city so people used to come to request him to take part in the agitations. He turned down their request saying "I do wish to be part of it but my children are small yet," and since he did not participate in the agitations, so the British conferred on him the Khan Bahadur title.

Iftikhar Arif : How were your meetings with Allama Iqbal?

Faiz: I saw Allama Sahab only once. There is a hazy picture of him in my memory. You must ask me when I spoke before an audience for the first time ... Anjuman Islamia celebrated its inception every year. All famous muslim leaders used to take part in that. Abba was President of Anjuman, I might have been four or five years old when I started memorising the Quran. I was chosen to recite Quran in the function. As soon as I climbed on the platform and began reciting, the secretary of Anjuman, Sheikh Zahoor Elahi Murad lifted me and put me on the *mansabar* (a special place on the platform). There I stood and recited the Quran for some time. So this was how my first public appearance took place.

Abba was a big man, he was vice-chairman of the district board, he held many such positions which I do not even remember. Whenever people like the deputy commissioner, commissioner or commander-in-chief came he would keep me with him and not Tufail (elder brother) or Inayat (younger brother) because by then I had begun to speak good English. Though I never enjoyed that, but that's how my exposure to public life happened at a very early stage in my life.

When I reached seventh-eighth standard a classmate of my brother Nazir Ahmed Mahmood who later became a judge, asked me, "you keep reading books of *shayari* (urdu poetry), have you ever written any *sher* yourself?" I said "No, I have not." Then he said, "There is a boy in my class Chhajju Ram, you write a *hajw* (satire) on him." I did whatever I could, wrong or right but wrote a *hajw* describing him that his head is like this, his stomach is like this, his legs look like this ... when he read the *hajw* he said "you are definitely a *shayar* (poet)"... next day he made the hajw popular in the entire school. I was very embarrassed with myself that Chhajju Ram might have taken offence at that. I did not even know him. I looked for him and offered my apology. He said, "I am rather happy that you have made me popular in the entire school. Why should you be sorry?"

So this was my first attempt at Urdu *Shayari*. Later when I reached the tenth standard, our teacher Bihari Lal gave us a *misra* (line of a verse) and asked us to complete it. Sayyad Mir Hasan was the judge. My *ghazal* was adjudged the best though I must say that the *ghazal* did not have any weight. Hasan Sahab became very happy and gave me one rupee as prize. This was the first prize of my life and I remember it vividly even today.

Iftikhar Arif : Tell us about your stint in Army. How did you join?

Faiz : When war began in 1939, my friends among political activists at that time held the view that it is a war of imperialism and that we do not have anything to do with it. Congress had launched the Quit India Movement and all Leftists, especially Communists and Socialists had been apprehended and put in Dalai camp. An elderly friend of mine Majid Mulk had joined Army as public relations officer and he insisted that I too should join the Army, but I turned down the request on the ground that it was a war of imperialism and I would not take part in it.

BBC at that time, started some programmes related to the ongoing war. Afzal, Sayyad uncle, Aijaz Badalwi joined BBC. ZB Bukhari used to be the in-charge then. They sent a telegram asking me to join BBC. At that time as a lecturer in a college in Amritsar, I used to earn Rs.120. I was tempted because there was this added attraction of going to London. I had not seen England till then though I had married an English lady. I did not have to go to England to marry her, she herself had come to Amritsar. There was also this desire that along with the job I would try to take admission in Cambridge or to become a barrister. But eventually after thinking over it from every angle I decided against it and sent a telegram that I would not side with imperialism in this war.

Then Germany attacked Russia and the Japanese nearly reached the borders of India. Our friends said it had now come down to saving our country, it was a World War, and that we would have to fight this war against fascism. On one of the evenings when I had gone for a discourse on radio, there was a call from Majid Mulk from Delhi. He said "you come to Delhi tomorrow, I have to discuss something with you." I understood what he would discuss with me. I consulted my friends and they all, readily approved the idea.

There, in Delhi, I was interviewed by an English Brigadier. He asked,

"A file on you from the CID is here on the table before me and it is written in this file that you are an advanced communist." I asked, “What is a retarded communist?” He said, “I do not care for this report, are you ready to work?” I said, "Yes, I will” ... this is how I joined the Army.

Iftikhar Arif : You had written some songs on the call given by Mahatma Gandhi?

Faiz : Yes, I was a trade union leader those days and had written many songs. For example, “Tujh ko manzoor ...”

[Translation from Urdu to English : Adil Muzaffar]

Syeda Hameed*

Remembering Faiz Sahab

It was the dead of winter. Alberta experiences the same temperatures during winter months as Siberia. A gloom descends throughout the Prairie region while the outdoor gets covered in a thick blanket of snow. I was living in Edmonton, coping with the exigencies of climatic rigour. I remember the date; it was November 28th, 1982 when I had got news that Faiz Sahab and Alys Faiz were coming to Edmonton. And as if that was not enough joy, they had agreed to let me host them in my house during their visit. During the next 3 days I saw the city come alive. It was as if spring had crept into the heart of winter. People went all out in welcome; they could not have enough of them. *Mehfils* were arranged, parties were organised and there were streams of visitors in my house.

Faiz Sahab sat on the sofa receiving visitors all day. He was mostly quiet, smiling through the visitations, the lit end of the cigarette, precariously balanced between his fingertips. I noticed that he looked tired from time to time, while Alys anxiously tried to introduce discipline in his routine. When he was pressed to recite his poetry, he used to come up with phrases such as, 'Okay, if you insist, I will recite a *ghazal* of Mehdi Hasan which you all love and never tire of hearing'.

> Tinting the blossoms, waft the spring breezes
>
> O come! So the garden transacts its daily business

At the time, I had not read much of Faiz Sahab's poetry apart from the texts of popular musical renderings. In 1984, I left Canada and returned to India to rediscover the roots I had left behind eighteen years ago. That is when I began to read and imbibe the poetry and philosophy of Faiz. The

---

*Syeda Hameed is a Member, Planning Commission, Govt. of India, New Delhi.

first thing to hit me was Faiz Sahib's identification with the masses not only of his country, but of the entire third world. This sentiment spans his entire poetic corpus, like the poem 'Aaj ke Naam' (Dedicated to Today) which is written for those on whose toil, the world rests. It is inscribed in his own handwriting as a dedication on the first page of the limited edition of his Complete Works.

Dedicated

To post men, to tonga wallahs

To rail men

To hungry youth toiling in factories

His cry was for freedom from all forms of exploitation. The best expression of this was in his *nazm,* written during the dark days of the Zia ul Haq regime. Immortalised by its musical rendering by Iqbal Bano, it has been sung by every renowned singer of the subcontinent and treated today as the Anthem for Freedom:

When dense mountains of oppression

Blow away like cotton clouds

When under the feet of the oppressed

Earth will shake, ground tremble

And over the heads of despots

Lightening will crackle

When crowns will be tossed up

And thrones will be demolished

We shall witness the day ordained.

He speaks to me as a voice for the world's oppressed, voiceless and suffering people. The world was his arena; for him *zulm* was *zulm,* regardless of where in the world it was perpetrated and on whom so ever it was wreaked. His poetry spoke out loud; whether it was for the Rosenbergs, in the Cold War of America in the 1950s, or for the Vietnam peasants, fleeing American napalm in 1960s. He wrote in protest against the repression of the Iranian students, the brutality on Palestinian children living in refugee camps and for the martyrs of North Africa.

Faiz Sahab was then in exile in Beirut. Once during a short visit to London, he asked his young friend Iftikhar Arif (who would later become a famous literary figure of the subcontinent) who ran a place for artists called Urdu Markaz, to dedicate his new poetic collection to Yasser Arafat. Its title was 'Mere dil, mere Musafir' (My heart, my traveller). The inspiration for this title, came from a couplet of the poet Dr. Iqbal which mirrored the mind of an exile, pining for his homeland and who had nothing to guide him with, in his grief but the hand of God.

Neither solace nor respite

The traveler has no hope except Allah

On March 5, 1951, Faiz was arrested under the Public Safety Act, charged with complicity in the Rawalpindi conspiracy case and sentenced to four years imprisonment. He stayed in Sargodha, Montgomery (now Sahiwal) Hyderabad and Karachi jails. Those were hard days of solitude when the pangs of separation from loved ones used to keep him awake at night. His letters from prison, to Alys have been published in 2011, by Sangmeel Publications, Lahore. Their title *Two Loves* speaks for itself. That was also the period when two of what would become his most popular collections appeared; 'Dast-e-saba' and 'Zindan Nama'. While he was staying with me I showed him, my well worn copy of 'Zindan Nama'. He wrote on it:

If it is a game of love play along, why fear

If you win what's better, if you lose the game's still yours

Looking back at the last three decades since his death, it strikes me that his most prophetic words were spoken at the time of accepting the Lenin Peace Prize in 1962. That was the time when the first Soviet scientist went into space and sent back his testimony to the world. These are Faiz words:

"Now that we can have a glimpse of our own planet from other stars,

> how foolish these small meanness acts appear, this desire to cut up the world into small parcels of land, this desire to dominate small groups of people. Isn't there even a handful of aware, honest and just human beings among us who can convince the others that since now the passageways to the entire universe are being opened up in front of our very eyes, and the riches of all creation are there for humanity to use we should dismantle all the military base and throw these bombs and rockets and guns into the sea, so that we may go forth together to conquer this wide universe where there is room enough for all mankind, where no one needs fight anyone else, where there is limitless peace and worlds without number."

He never lost hope; this man who Edward Said called 'One of the greatest poets of the 20th Century'. In many poems, Faiz celebrated the breaking of dawn after the blindness of night. My favourite are lines from the poem 'Dard aaye ga dabe paaoon' (Pain will come soft footed) written in 1954, from Montgomery jail. It begins with the poet himself struggling with his loneliness, within the walls of his prison. He says that at the lowest ebb of solitude, suddenly Pain (his faithful companion) will appear, bearing a red lamp which will light up the chambers of his heart. At the end, there is hope that beyond these walls, across the way, like- minded friends wait to join forces with prisoners like him.

Faiz Ahmed Faiz - Time Line

Name	Faiz Ahmed Khan
Literary Name	Faiz Ahmed Faiz
Date of Birth	13 February 1911
Place of Birth	Kala Qadir Town, District Sialkot
Father	Khan Bahadur Sultan Mohammad Khan
Mother	Sultan Fatima
Early Education	
1915	Began his education by memorising The Holy Quran at the age of four years
1916	He entered Moulvi Ibrahim Sialkoti's famous school for education - Arabic, Persian and Urdu
1921	He got admission to Class IV in Scotch Mission High School, Sialkot and passed with distinction
Secondary Education	
1927	Passed Matriculation in first division from the Punjab University
1929	Passed Intermediate in first division from Murray College, Sialkot
High Education	
1931	Passed BA (Honours) in Arabic from the Govern ment College, Lahore
1932	Passed MA (English Literature) with distinction from the Government College, Lahore

1933	Passed his MA in Arabic in the first division, from Oriental college, Lahore.
Teachers Saleem	Shamsul Ulema Meer Syed Hasan (Arabic), Yusuf Chishti (Urdu)
Syllabus Teachers	Ahmed shah Bukhari, Sufi Tabassum, Maulvi Mohammad Shafi
Literary Teachers	Dr Taseer, Maulana Salik, Maulana Chiragh Hasan Hasrat, Pundit Hari Chand Akhtar

Service and Other Engagements

1935	Lecturer in English at MAO College, Amritsar
1936	Took full part in the establishment of Progressive Writers' Association
1940	Appointed English teacher in Hailey College of Commerce, Lahore
1942	Joined the Army as Captain in 1942 and worked in the department of Public Relations in Delhi
1943	Was promoted to the rank of Major
1944	Was promoted to the rank of Lt. Colonel
1947	Resigned from the Army and returned to Lahore
1947-1951	Lahore Advisory Committee, Government of the Punjab
1951	Vice President, Pakistan Trade Union Federation
1948-1970	Member, Executive Council, World Peace Coun cil; President APP Trust
1959	Appointed as Secretary, Pakistan Arts Council and worked in that capacity till 1962
1964	Principal, Haji Abdullah Haroon College, Karachi

1964-1972	Vice President, Pakistan Arts Council, Karachi
1974-1977	Advisor, Cultural Affairs, Ministry of Education, Government of Pakistan
1958	Founder Member, Afro-Asian Literary Association

Editorship and Journalism

1938-39	Editor of monthly Adab-e-Latif, Lahore
1947-58	Chief editor of daily *Pakistan Times*, Lahore; daily Imroze, Lahore and weekly Lail-o-Nihar, Lahore
1978-84	Chief editor of Afro-Asian literary quarterly *Lo tus,* Beirut

Detention

1951	Arrested in Rawalpindi Conspiracy Case under Pakistan Safety Act on 9 March
1955	Released on 6 April
1958	Again arrested under Safety Act and was released in April 1959

Marriage

1941	Married to British born Miss Alys George. Sheikh Abdullah performed the Nikah rites
1942	First daughter Salima was born
1945	Second daughter Moneeza was born

Honours

1946	The British government conferred on him the title of MBE
1962	The Soviet government gave him the prestigious Lenin Peace Prize.

Books

Collection of Poems

1941	Naqsh-e-Faryadi
1952	Dast-e-Saba
1956	Zindan Nama
1965	Dast-e-Tahe Sang
1971	Sar-e-Wadi Seena
1978	Sham Shehar Yaran
1981	Mere Dil, Mere Musafir
1997	Nuskha Haiya Wafa

Collection of Prose Writing

1962	Meezan (essays in literary criticism)
1971	Saleebain mere dareeche main (letters)
	Muta-e-Lah-o-Qalam
1981	*Pakistan Times* Ke Idarye
1973	Moh-o-Saal; Ashnai (Travelogue)
	Safar Nama Cuba

Death

1984	On 20 November in Lahore

Faiz Ahmed Faiz with his grandson Adeel

Adeel Hashmi

From a grandson to his grandfather

Dearest Nana,

I was 11 years old when on that fateful night you were having a drink at our place, celebrating our parents' 17th wedding anniversary. Before the celebrations were over, you fell ill and had to be taken to the hospital. I wasn't allowed to go with you because I was too young. I was told nothing.

It was the next day when Salman Taseer and Aunty Chris came and hugged Mama (Alys Faiz) that I knew we'd never see you again. Not in person anyway.

The next day, which was the day of the funeral, it seemed to me as if the whole country had descended at our door step. I asked my elder brother how they all knew that Nana had died. He showed me the newspapers. It was the headlines of every single newspaper in Pakistan.

After you were gone there were some bad times and some very bad times for the people of Pakistan. Political victimisation, death threats, imprisonment and public lashings were common for anyone who dared to talk about art, free thinking, or anything against the current regime. I was young. But I remember.

I also remember a handful of progressive people, secretly gathering together for literary meetings and musical evenings, to celebrate your poetry.

When we went to school, your poetry was banned from our Urdu syllabus. That was 27 years ago.

Today the youth of this country, recites and relishes your poetry like never before.

As I write these lines, the year is 2011 and today those handful of people have grown into millions. Countless events are taking place in hundreds of cities across the world, to celebrate your 100th birthday.

They don't need to keep their love for you a secret anymore. The President of Pakistan and the President of India agree on very few things. One of them is you.

You once wrote a letter to Mama (Alys Faiz) from jail confiding that you had very few female friends and even fewer male friends. Today they cannot be counted.

You also have an equal number of followers; people who love, sing, narrate and cherish your poetry in several different languages spoken across the globe.

You always avoided talking about yourself. Even in your poetry, you never used the word 'I'. It was always 'We'. I wonder how you'd respond to so much love and affection being showered on you today.

I am fortunate and proud to belong to a generation that speaks and understands Urdu – the language that despite many great poets of the past, owes to you, perhaps, as much debt as a religion to its founder.

I am not young anymore, so I can share a drink with you now. We still need to finish the celebrations of that fateful evening, if not in person, then surely in spirit.

Adeel Hashmi
Model Town, Lahore
10 September, 2011

Acknowledgements

Celebrating Faiz Ahmed Faiz is an honour in itself, especialy during the hundredth year of his birth. We all acknowledge with reverence his contribution to world literature, culture and peoples' struggle. We are grateful to the authors from India and abroad who have contributed their articles in this volume through the *Think India Quarterly*. We are grateful to the Editorial Advisory Board and all those associated with the *Think India Quarterly* for publishing a special issue on the Faiz Centenary. Most of the articles in the book, are from this special issue .

We are grateful to the entire Faiz family, particularly Salima Hashmi, Moneeza Hashmi, Ali Madeeh Hashmi, Adeel Hashmi and Mira Hashmi.

The book could not have happened without my old friend Dharam Vir.

Our gratefulness would not be complete without thanking Mr. Sanjeev Ranjan for his hard work, dedication and most of the translations. We are thankful to Noor Zaheer for her guidance, help and translation of Faiz' play. I congratulate the publishers, specially P. K. Vij for the meticulous planning of the book, and all those associated with this book.

I take this opportunity to remind ourselves that life, civilizations and cultures are love, romance and revolution, and the world will ever remain grateful to Faiz, for all of it and more.

D. P. Tripathi
New Delhi

Index

www.ingramcontent.com/pod-product-compliance
Lightning Source LLC
Chambersburg PA
CBHW060606310726
48982CB00008B/1254/J